P9-DVB-841

TOWARDS A NEW
ARCHITECTURE

by

LE CORBUSIER

translated from the French

by

FREDERICK ETCHELLS

HOLT, RINEHART AND WINSTON

NEW YORK · TORONTO · LONDON · SYDNEY

BOOKS THAT MATTER

First published in the United States of America in 1960
by Praeger Publishers, Inc.
111 Fourth Avenue, New York. N.Y. 10003

Reprinted 1982, 1983

First published in England in 1927
by Architectural Press, London
All rights reserved
Library of Congress Catalog Card Number: 76–92371
ISBN 0-275-70990-6

Printed in USA

1 7 95

TOWARDS A NEW
ARCHITECTURE

Gregory Taylor
1985

THE TELEPHONE BUILDING, NEW YORK

PUBLISHERS' PREFACE

[To the 1946 edition]

THIS book has probably had as great an influence on English architectural thought as any one publication of the last fifty years. It first introduced the writings of Le Corbusier to the English reading public and was the first popular exposition in English of that "modern movement" in architecture which was gradually establishing itself on the Continent of Europe during the first quarter of this century and to which England was to make her own powerful contribution during the 'thirties. Of this movement Le Corbusier was—and still is—one of the principal prophets.

Apart from its intrinsic interest, which remains despite the lapse of twenty years, the book is therefore an important historical document. For this reason the present edition has been made an exact facsimile (slightly reduced in page size) of the original English edition, translated from the French by Mr. Frederick Etchells and published by John Rodker in 1927. It has been thought better, that is to say, to make no attempt to bring the contents up to date or to substitute later examples for the illustrations Le Corbusier originally chose to reinforce his arguments.

It should be added that Mr. Etchells's translation of 1927 was made from the thirteenth French edition, the book having originally been published in Paris in 1923, by Editions Crès, under the title *Vers Une Architecture*.

CONTENTS

ARGUMENT

THE ENGINEER'S ÆSTHETIC AND ARCHITECTURE

THE Engineer's Æsthetic, and Architecture, are two things that march together and follow one from the other : the one being now at its full height, the other in an unhappy state of retrogression.

The Engineer, inspired by the law of Economy and governed by mathematical calculation, puts us in accord with universal law. He achieves harmony.

The Architect, by his arrangement of forms, realizes an order which is a pure creation of his spirit ; by forms and shapes he affects our senses to an acute degree and provokes plastic emotions ; by the relationships which he creates he wakes profound echoes in us, he gives us the measure of an order which we feel to be in accordance with that of our world, he determines the various movements of our heart and of our understanding ; it is then that we experience the sense of beauty.

THREE REMINDERS TO ARCHITECTS

MASS

Our eyes are constructed to enable us to see forms in light.

.Primary forms are beautiful forms because they can be clearly appreciated.

Architects to-day no longer achieve these simple forms.

Working by calculation, engineers employ geometrical forms, satisfying our eyes by their geometry and our understanding by their mathematics ; their work is on the direct line of good art.

SURFACE

A mass is enveloped in its surface, a surface which is divided up according to the directing and generating lines of the mass ; and this gives the mass its individuality.

Architects to-day are afraid of the geometrical constituents of surfaces.

The great problems of modern construction must have a geometrical solution.

Forced to work in accordance with the strict needs of exactly determined conditions, engineers make use of generating and accusing lines in relation to forms. They create limpid and moving plastic facts.

PLAN

The Plan is the generator.

Without a plan, you have lack of order, and wilfulness

The Plan holds in itself the essence of sensation.

The great problems of to-morrow, dictated by collective necessities, put the question of " plan " in a new form.

Modern life demands, and is waiting for, a new kind of plan, both for the house and for the city.

REGULATING LINES

An inevitable element of Architecture.

The necessity for order. The regulating line is a guarantee against wilfulness. It brings satisfaction to the understanding.

The regulating line is a means to an end ; it is not a recipe. Its choice and the modalities of expression given to it are an integral part of architectural creation.

EYES WHICH DO NOT SEE

LINERS

A great epoch has begun.

There exists a new spirit.

There exists a mass of work conceived in the new spirit ; it is to be met with particularly in industrial production.

Architecture is stifled by custom.

The " styles " are a lie. —— superficiality —styles are not packaged architecture. They exclude the work of art.

Style is a unity of principle animating all the work of an epoch, the result of a state of mind which has its own special character.

Our own epoch is determining, day by day, its own style.

Our eyes, unhappily, are unable yet to discern it.

AIRPLANES

The airplane is the product of close selection.

The lesson of the airplane lies in the logic which governed the statement of the problem and its realization.

The problem of the house has not yet been stated.

Nevertheless there do exist standards for the dwelling house.

Machinery contains in itself the factor of economy, which makes for selection.

The house is a machine for living in.

AUTOMOBILES

We must aim at the fixing of standards in order to face the problem of perfection.

The Parthenon is a product of selection applied to a standard.

Architecture operates in accordance with standards.

Standards are a matter of logic, analysis and minute study ; they are based on a problem which has been well " stated." A standard is definitely established by experiment.

ARCHITECTURE

THE LESSON OF ROME

The business of Architecture is to establish emotional relationships by means of raw materials.

Architecture goes beyond utilitarian needs.

Architecture is a plastic thing.

The spirit of order, a unity of intention.

The sense of relationships; architecture deals with quantities.

Passion can create drama out of inert stone.

THE ILLUSION OF PLANS

The Plan proceeds from within to without; the exterior is the result of an interior.

The elements of architecture are light and shade, walls and space.

Arrangement is the gradation of aims, the classification of intentions.

Man looks at the creation of architecture with his eyes, which are 5 feet 6 inches from the ground. One can only deal with aims which the eye can appreciate, and intentions which take into account architectural elements. If there come into play intentions which do not speak the language of architecture, you arrive at the illusion of plans, you transgress the rules of the Plan through an error in conception, or through a leaning towards empty show.

PURE CREATION OF THE MIND

Contour and profile [1] are the touchstone of the architect. Here he reveals himself as artist or mere engineer.

Contour is free of all constraint.

There is here no longer any question of custom, nor of

[1] *Modénature*. I give the nearest equivalent of Le Corbusier's use of this word.—F. E.

tradition, nor of construction nor of adaptation to utilitarian
needs.

Contour and profile are a pure creation of the mind ;   they
call for the plastic artist.

MASS-PRODUCTION HOUSES

A great epoch has begun.

There exists a new spirit.

Industry, overwhelming us like a flood which rolls on
towards its destined ends, has furnished us with new tools
adapted to this new epoch, animated by the new spirit.

Economic law inevitably governs our acts and our
thoughts.

The problem of the house is a problem of the epoch.   The
equilibrium of society to-day depends upon it.   Architecture
has for its first duty, in this period of renewal, that of bringing
about a revision of values, a revision of the constituent elements
of the house.

Mass-production is based on analysis and experiment. standard.

Industry on the grand scale must occupy itself with building
and establish the elements of the house on a mass-production
basis.

We must create the mass-production spirit.

The spirit of constructing mass-production houses.

The spirit of living in mass-production houses.

The spirit of conceiving mass-production houses.

If we eliminate from our hearts and minds all dead concepts
in regard to the house, and look at the question from a critical

and objective point of view, we shall arrive at the " House-Machine," the mass-production house, healthy (and morally so too) and beautiful in the same way that the working tools and instruments which accompany our existence are beautiful.

Beautiful also with all the animation that the artist's sensibility can add to severe and pure functioning elements.

ARCHITECTURE OR REVOLUTION

In every field of industry, new problems have presented themselves and new tools have been created capable of resolving them. If this new fact be set against the past, then you have revolution.

In building and construction, mass-production has already been begun; in face of new economic needs, mass-production units have been created both in mass and detail; and definite results have been achieved both in detail and in mass. If this fact be set against the past, then you have revolution, both in the method employed and in the large scale on which it has been carried out.

The history of Architecture unfolds itself slowly across the centuries as a modification of structure and ornament, but in the last fifty years steel and concrete have brought new conquests, which are the index of a greater capacity for construction, and of an architecture in which the old codes have been overturned. If we challenge the past, we shall learn that " styles " no longer exist for us, that a style belonging to our own period has come about; and there has been a Revolution.

Our minds have consciously or unconsciously apprehended these events and new needs have arisen, consciously or unconsciously.

The machinery of Society, profoundly *out of gear*, oscillates between an amelioration, of historical importance, and a catastrophe.

The primordial instinct of every human being is to assure himself of a shelter. The various classes of workers in society to-day *no longer have dwellings adapted to their needs; neither the artizan nor the intellectual.*

It is a question of building which is at the root of the social unrest of to-day : architecture or revolution.

PONT DE GARABIT
Designed by Eiffel the engineer.

THE ENGINEER'S ÆSTHETIC
AND
ARCHITECTURE

The Engineer's Æsthetic and Architecture—two things that march together and follow one from the other—the one at its full height, the other in an unhappy state of retrogression.

The Engineer, inspired by the law of Economy and governed by mathematical calculation, puts us in accord with universal law. He achieves harmony.

The Architect, by his arrangement of forms, realizes an order which is a pure creation of his spirit; by forms and shapes he affects our senses to an acute degree, and provokes plastic emotions; by the relationships which he creates he wakes in us profound echoes, he gives us the measure of an order which we feel to be in accordance with that of our world, he determines the various movements of our heart and of our understanding; it is then that we experience the sense of beauty.

The Engineer's Æsthetic and Architecture—two things that march together and follow one from the other—the one at its full height, the other in an unhappy state of retrogression.

A QUESTION of morality; lack of truth is intolerable, we perish in untruth.

Architecture is one of the most urgent needs of man, for the house has always been the indispensable and first tool that he has forged for himself. Man's stock of tools marks out the stages of civilization, the stone age, the bronze age, the iron age. Tools are the result of successive improvement; the effort of all generations is embodied in them. The tool is the direct and immediate expression of progress; it gives man essential assistance and essential freedom also. We throw the out-of-date tool on the scrap-heap: the carbine, the culverin, the growler and the old locomotive. This action is a manifestation of health, of moral health, of *morale* also; it is not right that we should produce bad things because of a bad tool; nor is it right that we should waste our energy, our health and our courage because of a bad tool; it must be thrown away and replaced.

But men live in old houses and they have not yet thought of building houses adapted to themselves. The lair has been dear to their hearts since all time. To such a degree and so strongly that they have established the cult of the home. A *roof!* then other household gods. Religions have established themselves on dogmas, the dogmas do not change ; but civilizations change and religions tumble to dust. Houses have not changed. But the cult of the house has remained the same for centuries. The house will also fall to dust.

A man who practises a religion and does not believe in it is a poor wretch ; he is to be pitied. We are to be pitied for living in unworthy houses, since they ruin our health and our *morale*. It is our lot to have become sedentary creatures ; our houses gnaw at us in our sluggishness, like a consumption. We shall soon need far too many sanatoriums. We are to be pitied. Our houses disgust us ; we fly from them and frequent restaurants and night clubs ; or we gather together in our houses gloomily and secretly like wretched animals ; we are becoming demoralized.

Engineers fabricate the tools of their time. Everything, that is to say, except houses and moth-eaten boudoirs.

There exists in France a great national school of architecture, and there are, in every country, architectural schools of various kinds, to mystify young minds and teach them dissimulation and the obsequiousness of the toady. National schools !

Our engineers are healthy and virile, active and useful, balanced and happy in their work. Our architects are disillusioned and unemployed, boastful or peevish. This is because there will soon be nothing more for them to do. *We no longer have the money* to erect historical souvenirs. At the same time, we have got to wash !

Our engineers provide for these things and they will be our builders.

Nevertheless there does exist this thing called ARCHITECTURE, an admirable thing, the loveliest of all. A product of happy peoples and a thing which in itself produces happy peoples.   — Is this so true?

The happy towns are those that have an architecture.

Architecture can be found in the telephone and in the Parthenon. How easily could it be at home in our houses ! Houses make the street and the street makes the town and the town is a personality which takes to itself a soul, which can feel, suffer and wonder. How at home architecture could be in street and town !

The diagnosis is clear.

Our engineers produce architecture, for they employ a mathematical calculation which derives from natural law, and their works give us the feeling of HARMONY. The engineer therefore has his own aesthetic, for he must, in making his calculations, qualify some of the terms of his equation ; and it is here that taste intervenes. Now, in handling a mathematical problem, a man is regarding it from a purely abstract point of view, and in such a state, his taste must follow a sure and certain path.

Architects, emerging from the Schools, those hot-houses where blue hortensias and green chrysanthemums are forced, and where unclean orchids are cultivated, enter into the town in the spirit of a milkman who should, as it were, sell his milk mixed with vitriol or poison.[1]

People still believe here and there in architects, as they believe blindly in all doctors. It is very necessary, of course, that houses should hold together ! It is very necessary to have recourse to the man of art ! Art, according to Larousse, is the application of knowledge to the realization of a conception. Now, to-day, it is the engineer who *knows*, who knows the best way to construct, to heat, to ventilate, to light. Is it not true ?

Our diagnosis is that, to begin at the beginning, the engineer who proceeds by knowledge shows the way and holds the truth. It is that architecture, which is a matter of plastic emotion, should in its own domain BEGIN AT THE BEGINNING ALSO, AND SHOULD USE THOSE ELEMENTS WHICH ARE CAPABLE OF AFFECTING OUR SENSES, AND OF REWARDING THE DESIRE OF OUR EYES, and should dispose them in such a way THAT THE SIGHT OF THEM AFFECTS US IMMEDIATELY by their delicacy or their brutality, their riot or their serenity, their indifference or their interest ; these elements are plastic elements, forms which our eyes see clearly and which our mind can measure. These forms, elementary or subtle, tractable or brutal, work physiologically upon our senses (sphere, cube, cylinder, horizontal, vertical, oblique, etc.), and excite

[1] I have not felt it incumbent upon me to modify somewhat rhetorical passages such as the above.—F. E.

them. Being moved, we are able to get beyond the cruder
sensations ; certain relationships are thus born which work
upon our perceptions and put us into a state of satisfaction
(in consonance with the laws of the universe which govern
us and to which all our acts are subjected), in which man can
employ fully his gifts of memory, of analysis, of reasoning
and of creation.

Architecture to-day is no longer conscious of its own
beginnings.

Architects work in " styles " or discuss questions of structure in and out of season ; their clients, the public, still think
in terms of conventional appearance, and reason on the foundations of an insufficient education. Our external world has been
enormously transformed in its outward appearance and in the
use made of it, by reason of the machine. We have gained
a new perspective and a new social life, but we have not yet
adapted the house thereto.

The time has therefore come to put forward the problem of
the house, of the street and of the town, and to deal with
both the architect and the engineer.

For the *architect* we have written our " THREE REMINDERS."

MASS which is the element by which our senses perceive
and measure and are most fully affected.

SURFACE which is the envelope of the mass and which can
diminish or enlarge the sensation the latter gives us.

PLAN which is the generator both of mass and surface
and is that by which the whole is irrevocably fixed.

Then, still for the architect, " REGULATING LINES " showing by these one of the means by which architecture achieves that tangible form of mathematics which gives us such a grateful perception of order. We wished to set forth facts of greater value than those in many dissertations on the soul of stones. We have confined ourselves to the natural philosophy of the matter, *to things that can be known*.

We have not forgotten the dweller in the house and the crowd in the town. We are well aware that a great part of the present evil state of architecture is due to the *client*, to the man who gives the order, who makes his choice and alters it and who pays. For him we have written " EYES WHICH DO NOT SEE."

We are all acquainted with too many big business men, bankers and merchants, who tell us : " Ah, but I am merely a man of affairs, I live entirely outside the art world, I am a Philistine." We protest and tell them : " All your energies are directed towards this magnificent end which is the forging of the tools of an epoch, and which is creating throughout the whole world this accumulation of very beautiful things in which economic law reigns supreme, and mathematical exactness is joined to daring and imagination. That is what you do ; that, to be exact, is Beauty."

One can see these same business men, bankers and merchants, away from their businesses in their own homes, where everything seems to contradict their real existence—rooms too small, a conglomeration of useless and disparate objects, and a sickening spirit reigning over so many shams—Aubusson, Salon d'Automne, styles of all sorts and absurd bric-à-brac. Our industrial friends seem sheepish and shrivelled like tigers in a cage ; it is very clear that they are happier at their factories or in their banks. We claim, in the name of the steamship, of the airplane, and of the motor-car, the right to health, logic, daring, harmony, perfection.

We shall be understood. These are evident truths. It is not foolishness to hasten forward a clearing up of things.

Finally, it will be a delight to talk of ARCHITECTURE after so many grain-stores, workshops, machines and sky-scrapers. ARCHITECTURE is a thing of art, a phenomenon of the emotions, lying outside questions of construction and beyond them. The purpose of construction is TO MAKE THINGS HOLD TOGETHER ; of architecture TO MOVE US. Architectural emotion exists when the work rings within us in tune with a universe whose laws we obey, recognize and respect. When certain harmonies have been attained, the work captures us. Architecture is a matter of " harmonies," it is " a pure creation of the spirit."

To-day, painting has outsped the other arts.

It is the first to have attained attunement with the epoch.[1] Modern painting has left on one side wall decoration, tapestry and the ornamental urn and has sequestered itself in a frame— flourishing, full of matter, far removed from a distracting realism ; it lends itself to meditation. Art is no longer anec- dotal, it is a source of meditation ; after the day's work it is good to meditate.

[1] I mean, of course, the vital change brought about by cubism and later researches, and not the lamentable fall from grace which has for the last two years seized upon painters, distracted by lack of sales and taken to task by critics as little instructed as sensitive (1921).

On the one hand the mass of people look for a decent dwelling, and this question is of burning importance.

On the other hand the man of initiative, of action, of thought, the LEADER, demands a shelter for his meditations in a quiet and sure spot; a problem which is indispensable to the health of specialized people.

Painters and sculptors, champions of the art of to-day, you who have to bear so much mockery and who suffer so much indifference, let us purge our houses, give your help that we may reconstruct our towns. Your works will then be able to take their place in the framework of the period and you will everywhere be admitted and understood. Tell yourselves that architecture has indeed need of your attention. Do not forget the problem of architecture.

PISA

GRAIN ELEVATOR

THREE REMINDERS TO ARCHITECTS

I

MASS

Our eyes are constructed to enable us to see forms in light.

Primary forms are beautiful forms because they can be clearly appreciated.

Architects to-day no longer achieve these simple forms.

Working by calculation, engineers employ geometrical forms, satisfying our eyes by their geometry and our understanding by their mathematics; their work is on the direct line of good art.

GRAIN ELEVATOR

ARCHITECTURE has nothing to do with the various "styles."

The styles of Louis XIV, XV, XVI or Gothic, are to architecture what a feather is on a woman's head; it is sometimes pretty, though not always, and never anything more.

Architecture has graver ends; capable of the sublime, it

impresses the most brutal instincts by its objectivity; it calls into play the highest faculties by its very abstraction. Architectural abstraction has this about it which is magnificently peculiar to itself, that while it is rooted in hard fact it spiritualizes it, because the naked fact is nothing more than the materialization of a possible idea. The naked fact is a medium for ideas only by reason of the " order " that is applied to it. The emotions that architecture arouses spring from physical conditions which are inevitable, irrefutable and to-day forgotten.

Mass and surface are the elements by which architecture manifests itself.

Mass and surface are determined by the plan. The plan is the generator. So much the worse for those who lack imagination!

CANADIAN GRAIN STORES AND ELEVATORS

AMERICAN GRAIN STORES AND ELEVATORS

FIRST REMINDER : MASS

Architecture is the masterly, correct and magnificent play of masses brought together in light. Our eyes are made to see forms in light ; light and shade reveal these forms ; cubes, cones, spheres, cylinders or pyramids are the great primary forms which light reveals to advantage ; the image of these is distinct and tangible within us and without ambiguity. It is for that reason that these are *beautiful forms, the most beautiful forms.* Everybody is agreed as to that, the child, the savage and the metaphysician. It is of the very nature of the plastic arts.

Egyptian, Greek or Roman architecture is an architecture of prisms, cubes and cylinders, pyramids or spheres : the Pyramids, the Temple of Luxor, the Parthenon, the Coliseum, Hadrian's Villa.

Gothic architecture is not, fundamentally, based on spheres, cones and cylinders. Only the nave is an expression of a simple form, but of a complex geometry of the second order (intersecting arches). It is for that reason that a cathedral is not very beautiful and that we search in it for compensations of a subjective kind outside plastic art. A cathedral interests us as the ingenious solution of a difficult problem, but a problem of which the postulates have been badly stated beçause they do not proceed from the great primary forms. *The cathedral is not a plastic work; it is a drama; a fight against the force of gravity, which is a sensation of a sentimental nature.*

The Pyramids, the Towers of Babylon, the Gates of Samarkand, the Parthenon, the Coliseum, the Pantheon, the Pont du Gard, Santa Sophia, the Mosques of Stamboul, the Tower

really

But what are those?

of Pisa, the Cupolas of Brunelleschi and of Michael Angelo, the Pont-Royal, the Invalides—all these belong to Architecture.

The Gare du Quai d'Orsay, the Grand Palais do not belong to Architecture.

The *architects* of to-day, lost in the sterile backwaters of their plans, their foliage, their pilasters and their lead roofs, have never acquired the conception of primary masses. They were never taught that at the Schools.

Not in pursuit of an architectural idea, but simply guided by the results of calculation (derived from the principles which govern our universe) and the conception of A LIVING ORGANISM, *the* ENGINEERS *of to-day make use of the primary elements and, by co-ordinating them in accordance with the rules, provoke in us architectural emotions and thus make the work of man ring in unison with universal order.*

Thus we have the American grain elevators and factories, the magnificent FIRST-FRUITS *of the new age.* THE AMERICAN ENGINEERS OVERWHELM WITH THEIR CALCULATIONS OUR EXPIRING ARCHITECTURE.

COURTYARD   BRAMANTE AND RAPHAEL

THREE REMINDERS TO ARCHITECTS

II

SURFACE

A mass is enveloped in its surface, a surface which is divided up according to the directing and generating lines of the mass; and this gives the mass its individuality.

Architects to-day are afraid of the geometrical constituents of surfaces.

The great problems of modern construction must have a geometrical solution.

Forced to work in accordance with the strict needs of exactly determined conditions, engineers make use of generating and accusing lines in relation to forms. They create limpid and moving plastic facts.

ARCHITECTURE has nothing to do with the various "styles."

The styles of Louis XIV, XV, XVI or Gothic, are to architecture what a feather is on a woman's head; it is sometimes pretty, though not always, and never anything more.

SECOND REMINDER: SURFACE

Architecture being the masterly, correct and magnificent play of masses brought together in light, the task of the architect is to vitalize the surfaces which clothe these masses, but in such a way that these surfaces do not become parasitical, eating up the mass and absorbing it to their own advantage: the sad story of our present-day work.

To leave a mass intact in the splendour of its form in light,

but, on the other hand, to appropriate its surface for needs which are often utilitarian, is to force oneself to discover in this unavoidable dividing up of the surface the *accusing* and

generating lines of the form. In other words, an architectural structure is a house, a temple or a factory. The surface of the temple or the factory is in most cases a wall with holes for doors and windows; these holes are often the destruction of form; they must be made an accentuation of form. If the

essentials of architecture lie in spheres, cones and cylinders, the generating and accusing lines of these forms are on a basis of pure geometry. But this geometry terrifies the architects of to-day. Architects, to-day, do not dare to construct a Pitti Palace or a *rue de Rivoli;* they construct a *boulevard Raspail.*[1]

Let us base our present observations on the ground of actual needs : what we need is towns laid out in a useful manner whose general mass shall be noble (town planning). We have need of streets in which cleanliness, suitability to the necessities of dwellings, the application of the spirit of mass-production and industrial organization, the grandeur of the idea, the serenity of the whole effect, shall ravish the spirit and bring with them the charm that a happy conception can give.

[1] Or a Regent Street.—F. E.

To model the plain surface of a primary and simple form is to bring into play automatically a rivalry with the mass itself : here you have a contradiction of intention—the *boulevard Raspail*.

To model the surface of masses which are in themselves complicated and have been brought into harmony is to *modulate* and still remain within the mass : a rare problem—the *Invalides* of Mansard.

A problem of our age and of contemporary æsthetics : everything tends to the restoration of simple masses : streets, factories, the large stores, all the problems which will present themselves to-morrow under a synthetic form and under general aspects that no other age has ever known. Surfaces, pitted by holes in accordance with the necessities of their destined use, should borrow the generating and accusing lines of these simple forms. These accusing lines are in practice the chessboard or grill—American factories. But this geometry is a source of terror.

Not in pursuit of an architectural idea, but guided simply by the necessities of an imperative demand, the tendency of the engineers of to-day is towards the generating and accusing lines of masses ; they show us the way and create plastic facts, clear and limpid, giving rest to our eyes and to the mind the pleasure of geometric forms.

Such are the factories, the reassuring first fruits of the new age.

The engineers of to-day find themselves in accord with the principles that Bramante and Raphael had applied a long time ago.

N.B. Let us listen to the counsels of American engineers.
But let us beware of American architects. For proof:

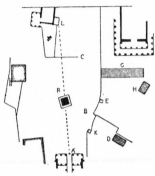

THREE REMINDERS TO
ARCHITECTS

III
PLAN

THE ACROPOLIS

A view which shows the Parthenon, the Erechtheum, and the statue of Athena in front of the Propylea. It should not be forgotten that the site of the Acropolis is very up and down, with considerable variations in level which have been used to furnish imposing bases or plinths to the buildings The whole thing being out of square, provides richly varied vistas of a subtle kind ; the different masses of the buildings, being asymmetrically arranged, create an intense rhythm. The whole composition is massive, elastic, living, terribly sharp and keen and dominating.

The *Plan* is the generator.

Without a plan, you have lack of order, and wilfulness.

The *Plan* holds in itself the essence of sensation.

The great problems of to-morrow, dictated by collective necessities, put the question of " plan " in a new form.

Modern life demands, and is waiting for, a new kind of plan both for the house and for the city.

ARCHITECTURE has nothing to do with the " styles."
It brings into play the highest faculties by its very abstraction. Architectural abstraction has this about it which is magnificently peculiar to itself, that while it is rooted in hard fact, it spiritualizes it. The naked fact is a medium for an idea only by reason of the " order " that is applied to it.

Mass and surface are the elements by which architecture manifests itself. Mass and surface are determined by the plan. The plan is the generator. So much the worse for those who lack imagination !

THIRD REMINDER : THE PLAN

The plan is the generator.

The eye of the spectator finds itself looking at a site composed of streets and houses. It receives the impact of the masses which rise up around it. If these masses are of a formal kind and have not been spoilt by unseemly variations, if the disposition of their grouping expresses a clean rhythm and not an incoherent agglomeration, if the relationship of mass to space is in just proportion, the eye transmits to the brain co-ordinated sensations and the mind derives from these satisfactions of a high order : this is architecture.

The eye observes, in a large interior, the multiple surfaces of walls and vaults ; the cupolas determine the large spaces ;

the vaults display their own surfaces; the pillars and the walls adjust themselves in accordance with comprehensible reasons. The whole structure rises from its base and is developed in accordance with a rule which is written on the ground in the plan : noble forms, variety of form, unity of the geometric principle. A profound projection of harmony : this is architecture.

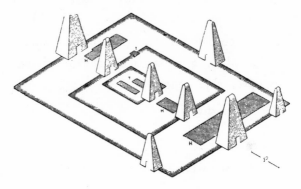

TYPE OF HINDOO TEMPLE
The towers make a rhythm in space.

The plan is at its basis. Without plan there can be neither grandeur of aim and expression, nor rhythm, nor mass, nor coherence. Without plan we have the sensation, so insupportable to man, of shapelessness, of poverty, of disorder, of wilfulness.

A plan calls for the most active imagination. It calls for the most severe discipline also. The plan is what determines everything ; it is the decisive moment. A plan is not a pretty thing to be drawn, like a Madonna face ; it is an austere abstraction; it is nothing more than an algebrization and a dry-looking thing. The work of the mathematician remains none the less one of the highest activities of the human spirit.

SANTA SOPHIA, CONSTANTINOPLE

The plan influences the whole structure : the geometrical laws on which it is based and their various modulations are developed in every part of the building.

Arrangement is an appreciable rhythm which reacts on every human being in the same way.

The plan bears within itself a primary and pre-determined rhythm : the work is developed in extent and in height following the prescriptions of the plan, with results which can range from the simplest to the most complex, all coming within the

same law. Unity of law is the law of a good plan : a simple
law capable of infinite modulation.

Rhythm is a state of equilibrium which proceeds either

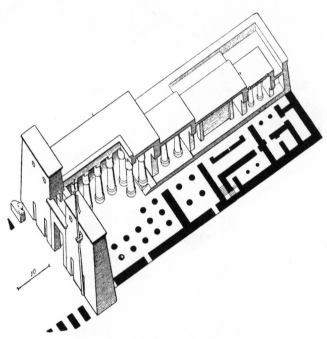

TEMPLE AT THEBES

*The plan is organized in accordance with the axis of the main entrance : the
Avenue of Sphinxes, the pylons, the courtyard and peristyle, the sanctuary.*

from symmetries, simple or complex, or from delicate
balancings. Rhythm is an equation ; Equalization (symmetry,
repetition) (*Egyptian and Hindoo temples*) ; compensation
(movement of contrary parts) (*the Acropolis at Athens*) ;
modulation (the development of an original plastic invention)

(*Santa Sophia*). So many reactions, differing in the main for every individual, in spite of the unity of aim which gives the rhythm, and the state of equilibrium. So we get the astonishing diversity found in great epochs, a diversity which is the result of architectural principle and not of the play of decoration.

The plan carries in itself the very essence of sensation.

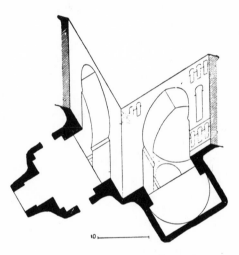

PALACE IN AMMAN (SYRIA)

But the sense of the plan has been lost for the last hundred years. The great problems of to-morrow, dictated by collective necessities, based upon statistics and realized by mathematical calculation, once more revive the problem of the plan. When once the indispensable breadth of vision, which must be brought to town planning, has been realized, we shall enter upon a period that no epoch has yet known. Towns must be

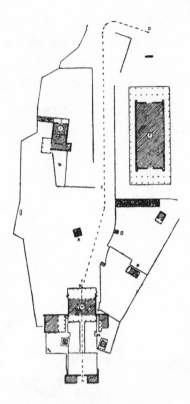

THE ACROPOLIS, ATHENS

The apparent lack of order in the plan could only deceive the unlearned. The balance of the parts is in no way a paltry one. It is determined by the famous landscape which stretches from the Piræus to Mount Pentelicus. The scheme was designed to be seen from a distance : the axes follow the valley and the false right angles are contrived with the skill of a first-rate stage manager. The Acropolis set on its rock and on its sustaining walls, seen from afar appears as one solid block. The buildings are massed together in accordance with the incidence of their varying plans.

conceived and planned throughout their entire extent in the same way as were planned the temples of the East and as the Invalides or the Versailles of Louis XIV were laid out.

The technical equipment of this epoch—the technique of finance and the technique of construction—is ready to carry out this task.

Tony Garnier, backed by Herriot at Lyons, planned his

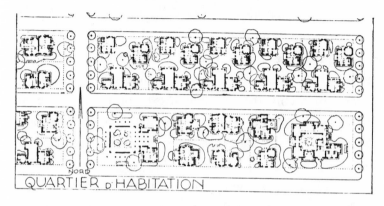

QUARTIER D'HABITATION

TONY GARNIER. A HOUSING SCHEME TAKEN FROM THE "CITÉ INDUSTRIELLE"

In his important studies on the Manufacturing Town, Tony Garnier has taken for granted certain possibilities of social development, not yet brought to pass, which would permit of methods of normal expansion of towns. The public would have complete control of all building sites. A house for each family : only one half of the area would be occupied by buildings, the other half being for public use and planted with trees : hedges and fences would not be allowed. In this way the town could be traversed in every direction, quite independently of the streets, which there would be no need for a pedestrian to use. The town would really be like a great park.

"industrial quarter" (*Cité*). It is an attempt at an ordered scheme and a fusion of utilitarian and plastic solutions. One fixed rule governing the units employed gives, in every quarter of the town, the same choice of essential masses and determines the intervening spaces in accordance with practical necessities and the biddings of a poetical sense peculiar to the architect. Though we may reserve our judgment as to the relationship of the various zones of this industrial city, one experiences here the beneficent results of order. Where order reigns, well-being begins. By the happy creation of a system of arrangement of the various plots, even the residential quarters for artisans take on a high architectural significance. Such is the result of a plan.

In the present state of marking time (for modern town planning is not yet born), the most noble quarters of our towns are inevitably the manufacturing ones where the basis of grandeur and style—namely, geometry—results from the problem itself. The plan has been a weak feature, and is still so to-day. True, an admirable order reigns in the interior of markets and workshops, has dictated the structure of machines and governs their movements, and conditions each gesture of a gang of workmen ; but dirt infects their surroundings, and incoherence ran riot when the rule and square dictated the placing of the buildings, spreading them about in a crazy, costly and dangerous way.

It would have been enough if there had been a plan. And one day we shall have a plan for our needs. The extent of the evil will bring us to this.

One day Auguste Perret created the phrase : " The City of Towers." A glittering epithet which aroused the poet in us. A word which struck the note of the moment because the fact itself is imminent ! Almost unknown to us, the " great city " is engendering its plan. This plan may well be a gigantic affair, since the great city is a rising tide. It is time that we

TONY GARNIER. DRAWING SHOWING THE PASSAGES OR WALKS
BETWEEN THE HOUSES

TONY GARNIER. A STREET IN A HOUSING SCHEME

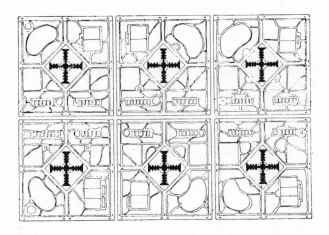

LE CORBUSIER, 1920. A CITY OF TOWERS

A project for Apartments or Flats, built as towers of 60 storeys and rising to a height of 700 feet ; the distance between the towers would be from 250 to 300 yards. The towers would be from 500 to 600 feet through their greatest breadth. In spite of the great area devoted to the surrounding parks, the density of a normal town of to-day is multiplied many times over. It is evident that such buildings would necessarily be devoted exclusively to business offices and that their proper place would therefore be in the centre of great cities, with a view to eliminating the appalling congestion of the main arteries. Family life would hardly be at home in them, with their prodigious mechanism of lifts. The figures are terrifying, pitiless but magnificent : giving each employee a superficial area of 10 sq. yds., a skyscraper 650 feet in breadth would house 40,000 people.

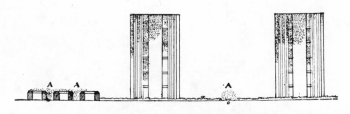

A CITY OF TOWERS

This section shows on the left how dust, smells, and noise stifle our towns of to-day. The towers, on the other hand, are far removed from all this and set in clean air amidst trees and grass. Indeed the whole town is " verdure clad."

LE CORBUSIER, 1923.   A CITY OF TOWERS

The towers are placed amidst gardens and playing-fields.   The main arteries, with their motor-tracks built over them, allow of easy, or rapid, or very rapid circulation of traffic.

should repudiate the existing lay-out of our towns, in which the congestion of buildings grows greater, interlaced by narrow streets full of noise, petrol fumes and dust ; and where on each storey the windows open wide on to this foul confusion. The great towns have become too dense for the security of their inhabitants and yet they are not sufficiently dense to meet the new needs of " modern business."

If we take as our basis the vital constructional event which the American sky-scraper has proved to be, it will be sufficient to bring together at certain points (relatively distant) the great density of our modern populations and to build at these points enormous constructions of 60 storeys high. Reinforced concrete and steel allow of this audacity and lend themselves in particular to a certain development of the façade by means of which all the windows have an uninterrupted view : in this way, in the future, inside courts and " wells " will no longer exist. Starting from the fourteenth storey you have absolute calm and the purest air.

In these towers which will shelter the worker, till now stifled in densely packed quarters and congested streets, all the necessary services, following the admirable practice in America, will be assembled, bringing efficiency and economy of time and effort, and as a natural result the peace of mind which is so necessary. These towers, rising up at great distances from one another, will give by reason of their height the same accommodation that has up till now been spread out over the superficial area ; they will leave open enormous spaces in which would run, well away from them, the noisy arterial roads, full of a traffic which becomes increasingly rapid. At the foot of the towers would stretch the parks : trees covering the whole town. The setting out of the towers would form imposing avenues ; there indeed is an architecture worthy of our time.

Auguste Perret set forth the principle of the City of Towers ; but he has not produced any designs. On the other hand he allowed himself to be interviewed by a reporter of the " Intransigeant " and to be so far carried away as to swell out his conception beyond reasonable limits. In this way he threw a veil of dangerous futurism over what was a sound idea. The reporter noted that enormous bridges would link each

tower to the next ; for what purpose ? The arteries for traffic
would be placed far away from the houses ; and the inhabitants, free to disport themselves in the parks among trees
planted in ordered patterns, or on the grass or in the places
of amusement, would never have the slightest desire to take
their exercise on giddy bridges, with nothing at all to do when
they got there ! The reporter would have it also that the

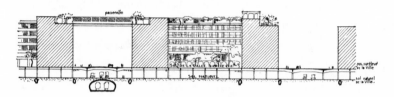

LE CORBUSIER, 1915. TOWNS BUILT ON PILES

*The ground level of the town is raised from 12 to 16 feet by means of concrete
piles which serve as foundations for the houses. The actual " ground " of the
town is a sort of floor, the streets and pavements as it were bridges. Beneath
this floor and directly accessible are placed all the main services, at present
buried in the ground and inaccessible—water, gas, electricity, telephone wires,
sewers, etc.*

town would be raised on innumerable piles of reinforced concrete carrying the streets at a height of 65 feet (6 storeys if you
please !) and linking the towers one to another. These piles
would leave an immense space underneath the town in which
would be placed the gas and water mains and the sewers, the
viscera of the city. Perret had never set out his plan, and the
idea could not be carried further without a plan.

I had myself put forward this idea of using piles a long
time before Auguste Perret, and it was a conception of a

much less grandiose character ; but it was capable of meeting a genuine need. I applied it to the existing type of town such as the Paris of to-day. Instead of forming foundations by excavating and constructing thick foundation walls, instead of digging up and digging up again the roadways in order to bury in them (a labour of Sisyphus) the gas and water mains, the sewers and the Tubes, with constant repairs to execute, it would be agreed that any new districts should be constructed at ground level, the foundations being replaced by the necessary number of concrete piles ; these would have carried the ground floor of the houses and, by a system of corbelling, the pavements and the roadways.

Within this space so gained, of a height of from 12 to 18 feet, would run heavy lorries, and the Tubes replacing the encumbrance of tramways, and so on, with a direct service to points immediately below the buildings. This complete network of traffic, working independently of that reserved for pedestrians and quick-moving vehicles, would be a pure gain and would have its own geography independent of any obstruction due to the houses : an ordered forest of pillars in the midst of which the town would exchange its merchandise, bring in its food supplies, and perform all the slow and clumsy tasks which to-day impede the speed of traffic.

Cafes and places for recreation would no longer be that fungus which eats up the pavements of Paris : they would be transferred to the flat roofs, as would be all commerce of a luxury kind (for is it not really illogical that one entire superficies of a town should be unused and reserved for a flirtation

between the tiles and the stars ?). Short passage-ways in the
shape of bridges above the ordinary streets would enable
foot traffic to get about among these newly gained quarters
consecrated to leisure amidst flowers and foliage.

The result of this conception would be nothing less than
a triplication of the traffic area of a town ; it was capable of
realization *since it corresponded to a need, was less costly
and more rational than the aberrations of to-day.* It was a
reasonable notion, given the old framework of our towns,
just as the conception of the City of Towers will prove a
reasonable idea, as regards the towns of to-morrow.

Here, then, we have a lay-out of streets which would bring
about an entirely new system of town planning and would
provide a radical reform in the tenanted house or apartment ; this
imminent reform, necessitated by the transformation of domestic
economy, demands a new type of plan for dwelling-houses,
and an entirely new organisation of services corresponding
to modern life in a great city. Here again the plan is the
generator ; without it poverty, disorder, wilfulness reign
supreme.

Instead of our towns being laid out in massive quadrangles,
with the streets in narrow trenches walled in by seven-storeyed
buildings set perpendicular on the pavement and enclosing
unhealthy courtyards, airless and sunless wells, our new lay-
out, employing the same area and housing the same number of
people, would show great blocks of houses with successive
set-backs, stretching along arterial avenues. No more courtyards, but flats opening on every side to air and light, and

LE CORBUSIER, 1920.   STREETS WITH SET-BACKS

Vast airy and sunlit spaces on which all windows would open.   Gardens and playgrounds around the buildings.   Simple façades with immense bays.   The successive projections give play of light and shade, and a feeling of richness is achieved by the scale of the main lines of the design and by the vegetation seen against the geometrical background of the façades.   Obviously we have here, as in the case of the City of Towers, a question of enterprise on a huge financial scale, capable of undertaking the construction of entire quarters.   A street such as this would be designed by a single architect to obtain unity, grandeur, dignity and economy.

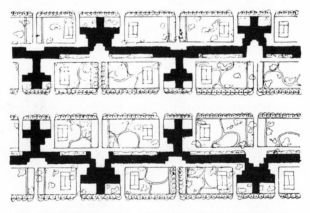

LE CORBUSIER, 1920.   STREETS WITH SET-BACKS

looking, not on the puny trees of our boulevards of to-day, but upon green sward, sports grounds and abundant plantations of trees.

The jutting prows of these great blocks would break up the long avenues at regular intervals. The various set-backs would promote the play of light and shade, so necessary to architectural expression.

Reinforced concrete has brought about a revolution in the æsthetics of construction. By suppressing the roof and replacing it by terraces, reinforced concrete is leading us to a new æsthetic of the plan, hitherto unknown. These set-backs and recessions are quite possible and will, in the future, lead to a play of half-lights and of heavy shade with the accent running not from top to bottom, but horizontally from left to right.

This is a modification of the first importance in the æsthetic of the plan ; it has not yet been realized ; but we shall be wise to bear this in our minds, in considering projects for the extension of our towns.

*   *   *

We are living in a period of reconstruction and of adaptation to new social and economic conditions. In rounding this Cape Horn the new horizons before us will only recover the grand line of tradition by a complete revision of the methods in vogue and by the fixing of a new basis of construction established in logic.

In architecture the old bases of construction are dead. We shall not rediscover the truths of architecture until new bases have established a logical ground for every architectural manifestation. A period of 20 years is beginning which will be occupied in creating these bases. A period of great problems, a period of analysis, of experiment, a period also of great æsthetic confusion, a period in which a new æsthetic will be elaborated.

We must study the *plan*, the key of this evolution.

LE CORBUSIER AND PIERRE JEANNERET.   A ROOF GARDEN ON A
PRIVATE HOUSE AT AUTEUIL

THE PORTE SAINT-DENIS (BLONDEL)

REGULATING LINES

An inevitable element of Architecture.

The necessity for order. The regulating line is a guarantee against wilfulness. It brings satisfaction to the understanding.

The regulating line is a means to an end; it is not a recipe. Its choice and the modalities of expression given to it are an integral part of architectural creation.

PRIMITIVE man has brought his chariot to a stop, he decides that here shall be his native soil. He chooses a glade, he cuts down the trees which are too close, he levels the earth around ; he opens up the road which will carry him to the river or to those of his tribe whom he has just left ; he drives in the stakes which are to steady his tent. He surrounds this tent with a palisade in which he arranges a doorway. The road is as straight as he can manage it with his implements, his arms and his time. The pegs of his tent describe a square, a hexagon or an octagon. The palisade forms a rectangle whose four angles are equal. The door of his hut is on the axis of the enclosure—and the door of the enclosure faces exactly the door of the hut.

The men of the tribe have decided to form a shelter for their god. They place him in a spot where they have made a clearing, properly laid out ; they put him under cover in a substantial hut and they drive in the pegs of the hut to form a square, a hexagon, or an octagon. They protect the hut by a solid palisade and drive in the pegs to take the shrouding of the ropes attached to the tall posts of the fence. They mark out the space to be reserved for the priests and set up the altar and the vessels of sacrifice. They open up an entrance in the palisade and they place it on the axis of the door of the sanctuary.

You may see, in some archæological work, the representation of this hut, the representation of this sanctuary : it is

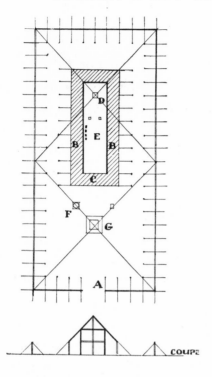

A PRIMITIVE TEMPLE

A. *Entrance.*
B. *Portico.*
C. *Peristyle.*
D. *Sanctuary.*
E. *Instruments of worship.*
F. *Vase of oblation.*
G. *Altar.*

the plan of a house, or the plan of a temple. It is the same
spirit that one finds again in the Pompeian house. It is the
spirit indeed of the Temple of Luxor.

There is no such thing as primitive man ; there are
primitive resources. The idea is constant, in full sway from
the beginning.

Note in these plans that they are governed by elementary
mathematical calculation. They are the product of measurement. In order to construct well and distribute your efforts
to advantage, in order to obtain solidity and utility in the
work, units of measure are the first condition of all. The

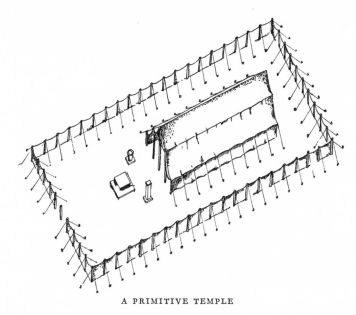

A PRIMITIVE TEMPLE

builder takes as his measure what is easiest and most constant, the tool that he is least likely to lose : his pace, his foot, his elbow, his finger.

In order to construct well and distribute his efforts to advantage, to obtain solidity and utility in the work, he has taken measures, he has adopted a unit of measurement, *he has regulated his work*, he has brought in order. For, all around him, the forest is in disorder with its creepers, its briars and the tree-trunks which impede him and paralyse his efforts.

He has imposed order by means of measurement. In order to get his measurement he has taken his pace, his foot, his elbow or his finger. By imposing the order of his foot or his arm, he has created a unit which regulates the whole work ; and this work is on his own scale, to his own proportion, comfortable for him, *to his measure*. It is on the human *scale*. It is in harmony with him : that is the main point.

But in deciding the form of the enclosure, the form of the hut, the situation of the altar and its accessories, he has had by instinct recourse to right angles—axes, the square, the circle. For he could not create anything otherwise which would give him the feeling that he was creating. For all these things—axes, circles, right angles—are geometrical truths, and give results that our eye can measure and recognize ; whereas otherwise there would be only chance, irregularity and capriciousness. Geometry is the language of man.

But in deciding the relative distances of the various objects, he has discovered rhythms, rhythms apparent to the eye and clear in their relations with one another. And these rhythms are at the very root of human activities. They resound in man by an organic inevitability, the same fine inevitability which causes the *tracing out of the Golden Section* by children, old men, savages and the learned.

A unit gives measure and unity ; a regulating line is a basis of construction and a satisfaction.

*   *   *

Is it not true that most architects to-day have forgotten that great architecture is rooted in the very beginnings of humanity and that it is a direct function of human instinct ?

When one looks at the little houses of the Paris suburbs, the villas on the Normandy dunes, the modern boulevards and the International Exhibitions, do they not convince us that architects are inhuman creatures, outside the common order, removed from our own nature and labouring perhaps for some other planet ?

It is because they have been taught a strange calling which consists in making other people—masons, carpenters and joiners—perform miracles of perseverance, care and skill in order to erect and stick together elements (roofs, walls, windows, doors, etc.) which have nothing in common and which have in truth for aim and consequence that of being designed for no useful purpose whatever.

*   *   *

For this reason, the world is unanimous in considering as dangerous gas-bags, shirkers, incapables, dull and hidebound characters, the one or two people who have grasped the lesson of primitive man in his glade, and who claim that there do exist such things as regulating lines : " With your regulating lines you kill imagination, you make a god of a recipe."

" But all earlier epochs have employed this necessary instrument."

" It is not true, you have invented it ; you are a maniac."

" But the past has left us proofs, iconographical documents, steles, slabs, incised stones, parchments, manuscripts, printed matter. . . ."

*   *   *

Architecture is the first manifestation of man creating his own universe, creating it in the image of nature, submitting to the laws of nature, the laws which govern our own nature, our universe. The laws of gravity, of statics and of dynamics, impose themselves by a *reductio ad absurdum :* everything must hold together or it will collapse.

A supreme determinism illuminates for us the creations of nature and gives us the security of something poised and reasonably made, of something infinitely modulated, evolved, varied and unified.

The primordial physical laws are simple and few in number. The moral laws are simple and few in number.

*   *   *

The man of to-day planes to perfection a board with a planing machine, in a few seconds. The man of yesterday planed a board reasonably well with a plane. Very primitive man squared a board very badly with a flint or a knife. Very primitive man employed a unit of measurement and regulating lines in order to make his task easier. The Greek, the Egyptian, Michaelangelo or Blondel employed regulating lines in order to correct their work and for the satisfaction of their artist's sense and of their mathematical thought. The man of to-day employs nothing at all and the result is the *boulevard Raspail.* But he proclaims that he is a free poet and that his instincts suffice ; but these can only express themselves by means of tricks learnt in the schools. A lyrical poet let loose with a halter round his neck, a man who knows things, but only things that he has neither discovered for himself nor even checked, a man who has lost, through all the teaching he has received, the ingenuous and vital energy of the child who never tires of asking " Why ? "

A regulating line is an assurance against capriciousness: it is a means of verification which can ratify all work created in a fervour, the schoolboy's rule of nine, the Q.E.D. of the mathematician.

The regulating line is a satisfaction of a spiritual order which leads to the pursuit of ingenious and harmonious relations. It confers on the work the quality of rhythm.

The regulating line brings in this tangible form of mathematics which gives the reassuring perception of order. The choice of a regulating line fixes the fundamental geometry of the work; it fixes therefore one of the " fundamental characters." The choice of the regulating line is one of the decisive moments of inspiration, it is one of the vital operations of architecture.

*   *   *

Here are regulating lines which have served to make very beautiful things and which are the very reason why these things are so beautiful.

FROM THE MARBLE SLAB FOUND IN 1882:

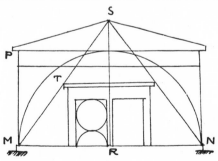

FAÇADE OF THE ARSENAL OF THE PIRÆUS

The façade of the Arsenal of the Piræus is " regulated " by a few simple divisions which give the proportion of the area to the height and fix the placing of the doors and their dimensions in intimate relationship with the actual proportions of the façade.

EXTRACT FROM A BOOK BY DIEULAFOY:

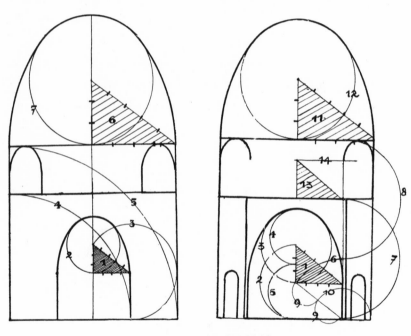

ACHÆMENIAN CUPOLAS

The great Achæmenian cupolas form one of the most subtle conclusions of geometry. Once the conception of the cupola was established in accordance with the poetical needs

of this race and of this epoch, and in accordance with the
static data of the constructive principles applied to it, the
regulating line comes in to rectify, correct, give point to and
pull together all the parts on the same unifying principle, that
of the triangle 3, 4, 5, which develops its effects from the
portico right up to the summit of the vault.

REGULATING LINES APPLIED TO NOTRE DAME, PARIS:

NOTRE DAME, PARIS

The determinant surface of the Cathedral is based on the
square and the circle.

REGULATING LINES SHOWN ON A PHOTOGRAPH OF THE
CAPITOL :

THE CAPITOL, ROME

The placing of the right angle has come into play to determine the intentions of Michaelangelo, causing the same principle,
which fixes the chief divisions of the wings and of the main
building, to govern the detail of the wings, the slope of the
staircases, the placing of the windows, the height of the
basement, etc.

The work is conceived in regard to its situation, and its
enveloping mass has been brought into association with the
volume and space of its surroundings ; it heaps itself together,

is concentrated, is a unit, expresses the same law throughout and becomes a massive thing.

EXTRACT FROM BLONDEL'S OWN NOTES ON THE PORTE SAINT DENIS

(See the illustration at the beginning of this section):

The principal mass is fixed, the opening of the bay is sketched in. A bold regulating line, on the unit of 3, divides the ensemble of the arch, and the various other parts of the work, as to height and breadth, and governs everything according to the same unit of 3.

THE PETIT TRIANON:

THE PETIT TRIANON, VERSAILLES

Placing of the right angle.

CONSTRUCTION OF A VILLA.   1916:

The general mass of the façades, both front and rear, is based on the same angle (A) which determines a diagonal whose many parallels and their perpendiculars give the measure

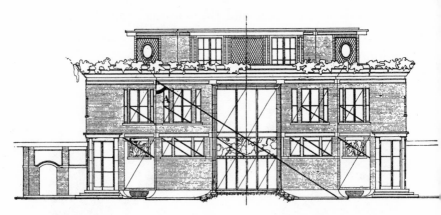

LE CORBUSIER, 1916.   A VILLA

for correcting the secondary elements, doors, windows, panels, etc., down to the smallest detail.

This villa of small dimensions, seen in the midst of other buildings erected without a rule, gives the effect of being more monumental, and of another order.

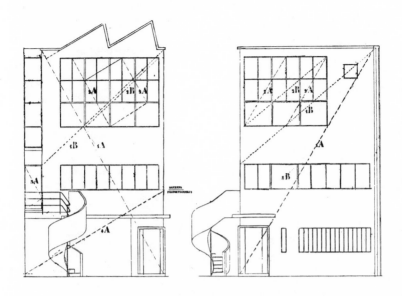

LE CORBUSIER AND PIERRE JEANNERET, 1923.   A HOUSE

LE CORBUSIER, 1916. A VILLA, BACK ELEVATION

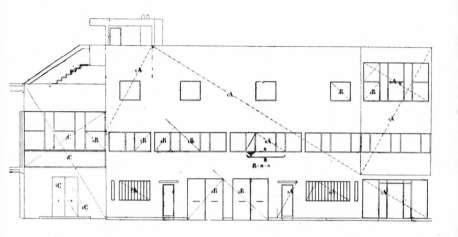

LE CORBUSIER AND PIERRE JEANNERET, 1924.   TWO HOUSES AT
AUTEUIL

THE " FLANDRE " (CIE. TRANSATLANTIQUE)

EYES WHICH DO NOT SEE

I

LINERS

A great epoch has begun.

There exists a new spirit.

There exists a mass of work conceived in the new spirit ; it is to be met with particularly in industrial production.

Architecture is stifled by custom.

The " styles " are a lie.

Style is a unity of principle animating all the work of an epoch, the result of a state of mind which has its own special character.

Our own epoch is determining, day by day, its own style.

Our eyes, unhappily, are unable yet to discern it.

There is a new spirit: it is a spirit of construction and of synthesis guided by a clear conception.

Whatever may be thought of it, it animates to-day the greater part of human activity.

A GREAT EPOCH IS BEGINNING

Programme of *l'Esprit Nouveau.*

No. 1. October 1920.

Nobody to-day can deny the æsthetic which is disengaging itself from the creations of modern industry. More and more buildings and machines are growing up, in which the proportions, the play of their masses and the materials used are of such a kind that many of them are real works of art, for they are based on " number," that is to say, on order. Now, the specialized persons who make up the world of industry and business and who live, therefore, in this virile atmosphere where indubitably lovely works are created, will tell themselves that they are far removed from any æsthetic activity. They are wrong, *for they are among the most active creators of contemporary æsthetics.* Neither artists nor business men take this into account. It is in general artistic production that the style of an epoch is found and not, as is too often supposed, in certain productions of an ornamental kind, mere superfluities which overload the system of thought which alone furnishes the elements of a style. Grotto-work does not make Louis Quinze, the lotus is not the Egyptian style, etc., etc.

From a tract issued by
l'Esprit Nouveau.

THE " decorative arts " are going strong ! After 30 years of underground work they are at their height. Enthusiastic commentators talk of *regenerating French art !* All we need remember of this adventure (which will finish badly) is that something more is being born than a rebirth of decoration : a new epoch is replacing a dying one. Machinery, a new factor in human affairs, has aroused a new spirit. An epoch creates its own architecture, and this is the clear image of a system of thought. During the topsy-turvydom of this critical period, till the arrival of a new age with its ideas set in order, clear and lucid, and with definite desires, decorative art was like the straw which drowning men are said to clutch at in a storm. A vain refuge ! Let us remember of this adventure that decorative art at least provided a good opportunity to unload the past and to feel our way once more towards the spirit of architecture. The spirit of architecture can only result from a particular condition of material things and a particular condition of mind. It would seem that events have succeeded one another sufficiently rapidly for a state of mind belonging to the period to assert itself and for the spirit of architecture to reach a formula. Even if the decorative arts are now at the dangerous height which goes before a fall, we may still say that men's minds to-day have been stirred up to remember what it is they aspire to. We may well believe that the appointed time of architecture has come.

M. PAUL VÉRA: TAIL PIECE

The Greeks, the Romans, the Grand Siècle, Pascal and Descartes, wrongly adduced as witnesses in favour of the decorative arts, have enlightened our judgment, and we now find ourselves immersed in architecture; architecture which is everything—but is not the " decorative arts."

Tail pieces and garlands, exquisite ovals where triangular doves preen themselves or one another, boudoirs embellished with " poufs " in gold and black velvet, are now no more than the intolerable witnesses to a dead spirit. These sanctuaries stifling with elegancies, or on the other hand with the follies of " Peasant Art," are an offence.

We have acquired a taste for fresh air and clear daylight.

*   *   *

Engineers unknown to the world at large, mechanics in

THE CUNARDER " AQUITANIA," WHICH CARRIES 3,600 PERSONS,
COMPARED WITH VARIOUS BUILDINGS

shop and forge have conceived and constructed these formidable affairs that steamships are. We land-lubbers lack the
power of appreciation and it would be a good thing if, to
teach us to raise our hats to the works of " regeneration,"
we had to do the miles of walking that the tour of a steamship
entails.

*   *   *

Architects live and move within the narrow limits of
academic acquirements and in ignorance of new ways of
building, and they are quite willing that their conceptions
should remain at doves kissing one another. But our daring
and masterly constructors of steamships produce palaces in
comparison with which cathedrals are tiny things, and they
throw them on to the sea !

Architecture is stifled by custom.

The use of thick walls, which was in earlier days a necessity,
has persisted, although thin partitions of glass or brick can
well enclose a ground floor with 50 storeys above it.

THE CUNARDER " AQUITANIA "

In a town like Prague, for example, an old enactment imposes a wall-thickness of 14 inches at the top storey of houses, with an additional projection of 4½ inches for each storey below, which means that the thicknesses of walls of buildings may easily be nearly 5 feet on the ground floor. To-day, the construction of facades in which soft stone is used in large blocks leads to this absurd result—that the windows, originally intended to introduce light, are flanked by deep embrasures which completely thwart the intention.

On the valuable ground of our great cities, you can still see masses of masonry rising as foundations for a building, although simple concrete piles would be equally effective.

THE "LAMORICIÈRE" (CIE. TRANSATLANTIQUE)

To architects : a beauty of a more technical order.   An æsthetic nearer to its real origins.

The roofs, these wretched roofs, still persist, an inexcusable paradox. The basements are still damp and cluttered up, and the service mains of our towns are invariably buried under stonework like atrophied organs, although a logical approach to the problem, easily realized, would produce the proper solution.

The "styles"—for he must indeed have something to furnish—come in as the great contribution of the architect. They intervene in the surface decoration of façades and of drawing-rooms ; this is the degeneration of "style," the old clothes of a past age ; it is a respectful and servile salute to the past : disquieting modesty ! It is a lie ; for in the " great periods " façades were smooth, pierced at regular intervals and of good human proportions. The walls were as thin as they dare make them. Palaces ? Very good for Grand Dukes of that time. But does any gentleman copy the Grand Dukes of to-day ? Compiègne, Chantilly, Versailles are good to behold from a certain angle, but . . . there is a great deal that might be said.

*　　　　*　　　　*

A house is a machine for living in. Baths, sun, hot-water, cold-water, warmth at will, conservation of food, hygiene, beauty in the sense of good proportion. An armchair is a machine for sitting in and so on.

Our modern life, when we are active and about (leaving out the moments when we fly to gruel and aspirin) has created its own objects : its costume, its fountain pen, its eversharp pencil, its typewriter, its telephone, its admirable office furniture, its plate-glass and its " Innovation " trunks, the safety razor and the briar pipe, the bowler hat and the limousine, the steamship and the airplane.

Our epoch is fixing its own style day by day. It is there under our eyes.

Eyes which do not see.

calls for reflection of contemporary situations.

We must clear up a misunderstanding : we are in a diseased state because we mix up art with a respectful attitude towards mere decoration. This is to displace the natural feeling for art and to mingle with it a reprehensible light-mindedness in

THE CUNARDER "AQUITANIA"

The same æsthetic as that of a briar pipe, an office desk or a limousine.

THE "AQUITANIA"

For architects : a wall all windows, a saloon full of light. What a contrast with the windows in our houses making holes in the walls and forming a patch of shade on either side. The result is a dismal room, and the light seems so hard and unsympathetic that curtains are indispensable in order to soften it.

THE LINER "FRANCE"

Made in the Saint-Nazaire yards. Good proportion. Look at this and think of some great buildings.

THE "AQUITANIA" (CUNARD LINE)

Architects note : a seaside villa, conceived as are these liners, would be more appropriate than those we see with their heavy tiled roofs. But perhaps it might be claimed that this is not a " maritime " style !

THE "AQUITANIA" (CUNARD LINE)

Architects note : the value of a " long gallery " or promenade—satisfying and interesting volume ; unity in materials ; a fine grouping of the constructional elements, sanely exhibited and rationally assembled.

THE " LAMORICIÈRE " (CIE. TRANSATLANTIQUE)

Architects note : new architectural forms ; elements both vast and intimate but on man's scale ; freedom from the " styles " that stifle us ; good contrast between the solids and voids ; powerful masses and slender elements.

THE "EMPRESS OF FRANCE" (CANADIAN PACIFIC)

An architecture pure, neat, clear, clean and healthy.   Contrast with this our carpets, cushions, canopies, wall-papers, carved and gilt furniture, faded or " arty " colours : the dismalness of our Western bazaar.

everything, which merely works to the advantage of the theories and campaigns conducted by " decorators " who do not understand their own period.

Art is an austere thing which has its sacred moments. We profane them. A frivolous art leers upon a world which has need rather of organisation, of implements and of methods and which is pushing forward in travail towards the establishment of a new order. A society lives primarily by bread, by the sun and by its essential comforts. Everything remains to be done ! Immense task ! And it is so imperative, so urgent

THE "EMPRESS OF ASIA" (CANADIAN PACIFIC)

" Architecture is the masterly, correct and magnificent play of masses brought together in light."

that the entire world is absorbed in this dominating necessity. Machines will lead to a new order both of work and of leisure. Entire cities have to be constructed, or reconstructed, in order to provide a minimum of comfort, for if this is delayed too long, there may be a disturbance of the balance of society. Society is an unstable thing and is cracking under the confusion caused by fifty years of progress which have changed the face of the world more than the last six centuries have done.

The time is ripe for construction, not for foolery.

The art of our period is performing its proper functions when it addresses itself to the chosen few. Art is not a popular thing, still less an expensive toy for rich people. Art is not an essential pabulum except for the chosen few who have need of meditation in order that they may lead. Art is in its essence arrogant.

*   *   *

In the painful gestation of this age as it forms itself, a need of harmony becomes evident.

May our eyes be opened : this harmony already exists, the result of work governed by *economy* and conditioned by physical necessities. This harmony has its causes ; it is not in any way the effect of caprice, but is of a logical construction and congruous with the world around it. In the daring transposition of human labour that has taken place, nature has still been present and with the greater rigour as the problem was difficult. The creations of mechanical technique are organisms tending to a pure functioning, and obey the same evolutionary laws as those objects in nature which excite our admiration. There is harmony in the performances which come from the workshop or the factory. It is not Art ; it is not the Sistine Chapel nor the Erechtheum ; these are the everyday jobs of a whole world working with perception, intelligence and precision, with imagination, daring and severity.

If we forget for a moment that a steamship is a machine for transport and look at it with a fresh eye, we shall feel that we are facing an important manifestation of temerity, of discipline, of harmony, of a beauty that is calm, vital and strong.

A seriously-minded architect, looking at it as an architect (*i.e.* a creator of organisms), will find in a steamship his freedom from an age-long but contemptible enslavement to the past.

He will prefer respect for the forces of nature to a lazy respect for tradition; to the narrowness of commonplace conceptions he will prefer the majesty of solutions which spring from a problem that has been clearly stated—solutions needed by this age of mighty effort which has taken so gigantic a step forward.

The house of the earth-man is the expression of a circumscribed world. The steamship is the first stage in the realization of a world organized according to the new spirit.

EYES WHICH DO NOT SEE

II

AIRPLANES

The airplane is the product of close selection.

The lesson of the airplane lies in the logic which governed the statement of the problem and its realization.

The problem of the house has not yet been stated.

Nevertheless there do exist standards for the dwelling house.

Machinery contains in itself the factor of economy, which makes for selection.

The house is a machine for living in.

There is a new spirit : it is a spirit of construction and of synthesis guided by a clear conception.

Whatever may be thought of it, it animates to-day the greater part of human activity.

A GREAT EPOCH HAS BEGUN

Programme of *l'Esprit Nouveau*.
No, 1.   October, 1920.

THERE is one profession and one only, namely architecture, in which progress is not considered necessary, where laziness is enthroned, and in which the reference is always to yesterday.

Everywhere else, taking thought for the morrow is almost a fever and brings its inevitable solution : if a man does not move forward he becomes bankrupt.

But in architecture no one ever becomes bankrupt. A privileged profession, alas !

*   *   *

The airplane is indubitably one of the products of the most intense selection in the range of modern industry.

The War was an insatiable " client," never satisfied, always demanding better. The orders were to succeed at all costs and death followed a mistake remorselessly. We may then affirm that the airplane mobilized invention, intelligence and daring : *imagination* and *cold reason*. It is the same spirit that built the Parthenon.

Let us look at things from the point of view of

architecture, but in the state of mind of the inventor of airplanes.

The lesson of the airplane is not primarily in the forms it has created, and above all we must learn to see in an airplane not a bird or a dragon-fly, but a machine for flying ; the lesson of the airplane lies in the logic which governed the enunciation of the problem and which led to its successful realization. When a problem is properly stated, in our epoch, it inevitably finds its solution.

The problem of the house has not yet been stated.

One commonplace among Architects (the younger ones) : *the construction must be shown.*

Another commonplace amongst them : *when a thing responds to a need, it is beautiful.*

But. . . . To show the construction is all very well for an Arts and Crafts student who is anxious to prove his ability. The Almighty has clearly shown our wrists and our ankles, but there remains all the rest !

When a thing responds to a need, it is not beautiful ; it satisfies all one part of our mind, the primary part, without which there is no possibility of richer satisfactions ; let us recover the right order of events.

Architecture has another meaning and other ends to pursue than showing construction and responding to needs (and by " needs " I mean utility, comfort and practical arrangement).

ARCHITECTURE is the art above all others which achieves a state of platonic grandeur, mathematical order, speculation,

the perception of the harmony which lies in emotional relationships. This is the AIM of architecture.

But let us return to our chronology.

If we feel the need of a new architecture, a clear and settled
organism, it is because, as things are, the sensation of mathematical order cannot touch us since *things no longer respond
to a need*, and because there is no longer real construction in
architecture. An extreme confusion reigns. Architecture as
practised provides no solution to the present-day problem of
the dwelling-house and has no comprehension of the structure
of things. It does not fulfil the very first conditions and so
it is not possible that the higher factors of harmony and beauty
should enter in.

AIR EXPRESS

FARMAN

The architecture of to-day does not fulfil the necessary and sufficient conditions of the problem.

The reason is that the problem has not been stated as regards architecture. There has been no salutary war as in the case of the airplane.

But you will say, the Peace has set the problem in the reconstruction of the North of France. But then, we are totally disarmed, we do not know how to build in a modern

SPAD 33 BLERIOT. PASSENGER PLANE
(*Designed by Herbemont.*)

way—materials, systems of construction, THE CONCEPTION OF
THE DWELLING, all are lacking. Engineers have been busy
with barrages, with bridges, with Atlantic liners, with mines,
with railways. Architects have been asleep.

The airplane shows us that a problem well stated finds its
solution. To wish to fly like a bird is to state the problem
badly, and Ader's " Bat " never left the ground. To invent a
flying machine having in mind nothing alien to pure mechanics,
that is to say, to search for a means of suspension in the air and
a means of propulsion, was to put the problem properly : in
less than ten years the whole world could fly.

TRIPLE HYDROPLANE CAPRONI
3,000 *h.p.   Capable of carrying* 100 *passengers.*

LET US STATE THE PROBLEM

Let us shut our eyes to what exists.

A house : a shelter against heat, cold, rain, thieves and the inquisitive. A receptacle for light and sun. A certain number of cells appropriated to cooking, work, and personal life.

A room : a surface over which one can walk at ease, a bed on which to stretch yourself, a chair in which to rest or work, a work-table, receptacles in which each thing can be put at once in its right place.

The number of rooms : one for cooking and one for eating. One for work, one to wash yourself in and one for sleep.

TRIPLANE CAPRONI

2,000 *h.p.   Can carry 30 passengers.*

Such are the standards of the dwelling.

Then why do we have the enormous and useless roofs on pretty suburban villas ? Why the scanty windows with their little panes ; why large houses with so many rooms locked up ? Why the mirrored wardrobes, the washstands, the commodes ? And then, why the elaborate bookcases ? the consoles, the china cabinets, the dressers, the sideboards ? Why the enormous glass chandeliers ? The mantelpieces ? Why the draped curtains ? Why the damasked wall-papers thick with colour, with their motley design ?

Daylight hardly enters your homes. Your windows are difficult to open. There are no ventilators for changing the

AIR EXPRESS

This does the journey from London to Paris in two hours.

air such as we get in any dining-car. Your chandeliers hurt
the eyes. Your imitation stone stucco and your wall-papers
are an impertinence, and no good modern picture could ever
be hung on your walls, for it would be lost in the welter of
your furnishings.

Why do you not demand from your landlord :

1. Fittings to take underclothing, suits and dresses in your
bedroom, all of one depth, of a comfortable height and as
practical as an " Innovation " trunk ;

2. In your dining-room fittings to take china, silver and
glass, shutting tightly and with a sufficiency of drawers in
order that " clearing away " can be done in an instant, and all
these fittings " built in " so that round your chairs and table

FARMAN "MOSQUITO"

you have room enough to move and that feeling of space which will give you the calm necessary to good digestion;

3. In your living-room *fittings to hold your books and protect them from dust and to hold your collection of paintings and works of art.* And in such a way that the walls of your room are unencumbered. You could then bring out your pictures one at a time when you want them.

As for your dressers, and your mirrored wardrobes, you can sell all these to one of those young nations which have lately appeared on the map. There *Progress* rages, and they are dropping the traditional home (with its fittings, etc.) to live in an up-to-date house *à l'européenne* with its imitation stone stucco and its mantelpieces.

Let us repeat some fundamental axioms:

(a) *Chairs are made to sit in.* There are rush-seated church chairs at 5s., luxuriously upholstered arm-chairs at £20 and

SPAD XIII BLERIOT

(*Designed by Bechneau.*)

AIR EXPRESS

Capable of 140 *m.p.h.*

FARMAN " GOLIATH." BOMBING MACHINE

adjustable chairs with a movable reading-desk, a shelf for your
coffee cup, an extending foot-rest, a back that raises and lowers
with a handle, and gives you the very best position either for
work or a nap, in a healthy, comfortable and right way. Your
bergères, your Louis XVI *causeuses*, bulging through their
tapestry covers, are these machines for sitting in ? Between
ourselves, you are more comfortable at your club, your bank
or in your office.

(b) *Electricity gives light.* We can have concealed lighting,
or we can have diffused and projected lighting. One can see
as clearly as in broad daylight without ever hurting one's eyes.

A hundred-candle-power lamp weighs less than two ounces,
but there are chandeliers weighing nearly two hundredweight
with elaborations in bronze or wood, and so huge that they
fill up all the middle of the room ; the upkeep of these horrors

is a terrible task because of the flies. These chandeliers are also very bad for the eyes at night.

(c) *Windows serve to admit light, " a little, much, or not at all," and to see outside.* There are windows in sleeping-cars which close hermetically or can be opened at will; there are the great windows of modern cafés which close hermetically or can be entirely opened by means of a handle which causes them to disappear below ground; there are the windows in dining cars which have little louvres opening to admit air " a little, much, or not at all," there is modern plate glass which has replaced bottle-glass and small panes; there are roll shutters which can be lowered gradually and will keep out the light at will according to the spacing of their slats. But architects still use only windows like those at Versailles or Compiègne, Louis X, Y or Z which shut badly, have tiny panes, are difficult to open and have their shutters outside; if it rains in the evening one gets wet through in trying to close them.

(d) *Pictures are made to be looked at and meditated on.* In order to see a picture to advantage, it must be hung suitably and in the proper atmosphere. The true collector of pictures arranges them in a cabinet and hangs on the wall the particular painting he wants to look at; but your walls are a riot of all manner of things.

(e) *A house is made for living in.*—" No ! "—" But of course ! "—" Then you are a Utopian ! "

Truth to tell, the modern man is bored to tears in his home; so he goes to his club. The modern woman is bored

AIR EXPRESS.   A FARMAN " GOLIATH "

outside her boudoir ; she goes to tea-parties. The modern
man and woman are bored at home ; they go to night-clubs.
But lesser folk who have no clubs gather together in the

evening under the chandelier and hardly dare to walk through the labyrinth of their furniture which takes up the whole room and is all their fortune and their pride.

The existing plan of the dwelling-house takes no account of man and is conceived as a furniture store. This scheme of things, favourable enough to the trade of Tottenham Court Road, is of ill omen for society. It kills the spirit of the family, of the home ; there are no homes, no families and no children, for living is much too difficult a business.

The temperance societies and the anti-Malthusians should address an urgent appeal to architects ; they should have the MANUAL OF THE DWELLING printed and distributed to mothers of families and should demand the resignation of all the professors in the architectural schools.

THE MANUAL OF THE DWELLING

Demand a bathroom looking south, one of the largest rooms in the house or flat, the old drawing-room for instance. One wall to be entirely glazed, opening if possible on to a balcony for sun baths ; the most up-to-date fittings with a shower-bath and gymnastic appliances.

An adjoining room to be a dressing-room in which you can dress and undress. Never undress in your bedroom. It is not a clean thing to do and makes the room horribly untidy. In this room demand fitments for your linen and clothing, not more than 5 feet in height, with drawers, hangers, etc.

Demand one really large living room instead of a number of small ones.

Demand bare walls in your bedroom, your living room and your dining-room. Built-in fittings to take the place of much of the furniture, which is expensive to buy, takes up too much room and needs looking after.

If you can, put the kitchen at the top of the house to avoid smells.

Demand concealed or diffused lighting.

Demand a vacuum cleaner.

Buy only practical furniture and never buy decorative " pieces." If you want to see bad taste, go into the houses of the rich. Put only a few pictures on your walls and none but good ones.

Keep your odds and ends in drawers or cabinets.

The gramophone or the pianola or wireless will give you exact interpretations of first-rate music, and you will avoid catching cold in the concert hall, and the frenzy of the virtuoso.

Demand ventilating panes to the windows in every room.

Teach your children that a house is only habitable when it is full of light and air, and when the floors and walls are clear. To keep your floors in order eliminate heavy furniture and thick carpets.

Demand a separate garage to your dwelling.

Demand that the maid's room should not be an attic. Do not park your servants under the roof.

Take a flat which is one size smaller than what your parents accustomed you to. Bear in mind economy in your actions, your household management and in your thoughts.

Conclusion. Every modern man has the mechanical sense. The feeling for mechanics exists and is justified by our daily

FARMAN "GOLIATH"

Paris to Prague in six hours.   Paris to Warsaw in nine hours.

THE PROBLEM BADLY CONCEIVED:

EYES WHICH DO NOT SEE . .

FARMAN

activities. This feeling in regard to machinery is one of respect, gratitude and esteem.

Machinery includes economy as an essential factor leading to minute selection. There is a moral sentiment in the feeling for mechanics.

The man who is intelligent, cold and calm has grown wings to himself.

Men—intelligent, cold and calm—are needed to build the house and to lay out the town.

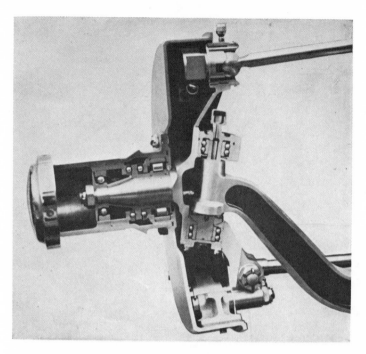

DELAGE. FRONT-WHEEL BRAKE

This precision, this cleanness in execution go further back than our re-born mechanical sense. Phidias felt in this way: the entablature of the Parthenon is a witness. So did the Egyptians when they polished the Pyramids. This at a time when Euclid and Pythagoras dictated to their contemporaries.

EYES WHICH DO NOT SEE

III

AUTOMOBILES

We must aim at the fixing of standards in order to face the problem of perfection.

The Parthenon is a product of selection applied to a standard.

Architecture operates in accordance with standards.

Standards are a matter of logic, analysis and minute study : they are based on a problem which has been well "stated."

A standard is definitely established by experiment.

DELAGE, 1921

If the problem of the dwelling or the flat were studied in the same way that a chassis is, a speedy transformation and improvement would be seen in our houses. If houses were constructed by industrial mass-production, like chassis, unexpected but sane and defensible forms would soon appear, and a new æsthetic would be formulated with astonishing precision.

There is a new spirit: it is a spirit of construction and of synthesis guided by clear conception.

Programme of *l'Esprit Nouveau.*
No. 1. October 1920.

IT is necessary to press on towards the establishment of *standards* in order to face the problem of *perfection*.

The Parthenon is a product of selection applied to an established standard. Already for a century the Greek temple had been standardized in all its parts.

PAESTUM, 600–550 B.C.

When once a standard is established, competition comes at once and violently into play. It is a fight; in order to win you must do better than your rival *in every minute point*, in

HUMBER, 1907

THE PARTHENON, 447–434 B.C.

the run of the whole thing and in all the details. Thus we get the study of minute points pushed to its limits. Progress.

A standard is necessary for order in human effort.

DELAGE, "GRAND-SPORT," 1921

HISPANO-SUIZA, 1911.   OZENFANT COACHWORK

A standard is established on sure bases, not capriciously but with the surety of something intentional and of a logic controlled by analysis and experiment.

All men have the same organism, the same functions.

All men have the same needs.

The social contract which has evolved through the ages fixes standardized classes, functions and needs producing standardized products.

The house is a thing essential to man.

Painting is a thing essential to man since it responds to needs of a spiritual order, determined by the standards of emotion.

All great works of art are based on one or other of the great standards of the heart: *Œdipus, Phædra,* the *Enfant Prodigue,* the Madonnas, *Paul et Virginie,* Philemon and Baucis.

BIGNAN-SPORT 1921

the *Pauvre Pêcheur,* the *Marseillaise, Madelon vient nous verser à boire.* . . .

The establishment of a standard involves exhausting every practical and reasonable possibility, and extracting from them a recognized type conformable to its functions, with a maximum output and a minimum use of means, workmanship and material, words, forms, colours, sounds.

The motor-car is an object with a simple function (to travel) and complicated aims (comfort, resistance, appearance), which has forced on big industry the absolute necessity of standardization. All motor-cars have the same essential arrangements. But, by reason of the unceasing competition between the innumerable firms who make them, every maker has found himself obliged to get to the top of this competition and, over and above the standard of practical realization, to prosecute the

search for a perfection and a harmony beyond the mere practical side, a manifestation not only of perfection and harmony,
but of beauty.

Here we have the birth of style, that is to say the attainment,
universally recognized, of a state of perfection universally felt.

The establishment of a standard is developed by organizing
rational elements, following a line of direction equally rational.
The form and appearance are in no way preconceived, *they
are a result ;* they may have a strange look at first sight.   Ader
made a " Bat," but it did not fly ; Wright and Farman set
themselves the problem of sustaining solid bodies in air, the
result was jarring and disconcerting, but it flew.   The standard
had been fixed.   Practical results followed.

The first motor-cars were constructed, and their bodies
built, on old lines.   This was contrary to the necessities of the
displacement and rapid penetration of a solid body.   The study
of the laws of penetration fixed the standard, a standard which
has evolved in accordance with two different aims : speed, the
greater mass in front (sporting bodies) ; comfort, the main bulk
at the back (saloon).   In either case there is no longer anything
in common with the ancient carriage with its slow displacement.

Civilizations advance.   They pass through the age of the
peasant, the soldier and the priest and attain what is rightly
called culture.   Culture is the flowering of the effort to select.
Selection means rejection, pruning, cleansing ; the clear and
naked emergence of the Essential.

From the primitiveness of the Early Christian chapel, we
pass to *Notre Dame* of Paris, the *Invalides,* the *Place de la*

THE PARTHENON

Little by little the Greek temple was formulated, passing from construction to Architecture. One hundred years later the Parthenon marked the climax of the ascending curve.

Concorde. Feeling has been clarified and refined, mere decoration set aside and proportion and scale attained, an advance has been made ; we have passed from the elementary satisfactions (decoration) to the higher satisfactions (mathematics).

If Breton cupboards still remain in Brittany, it is because the Bretons have continued there, very remote and very stable, fully occupied in their fishing and cattle breeding. It is not seemly that a gentleman of good standing should sleep on a Breton bed in his Paris mansion ; it is not seemly that a gentleman who owns a saloon car should sleep in a Breton bed, and

THE PARTHENON

Each part is decisive and marks the highest point in precision and execution :
proportion is clearly written therein.

so on. We have only to get a clear idea of this and to draw the logical conclusion. To own together a large car and a Breton bed is quite usual, I am sorry to say.

Everybody asserts with conviction and enthusiasm : " The motor-car marks the style of our epoch ! " but the Breton bed is sold and manufactured every day by the antique dealers.

Let us display, then, the Parthenon and the motor-car so that it may be clear that it is a question of two products of selection in different fields, one of which has reached its climax and the other is evolving. That ennobles the automobile. And what then ? Well, then it remains to use the motor-car

TRIPLE HYDROPLANE. CAPRONI
Showing how plastic organisms are created in response to a well-stated problem.

as a challenge to our houses and our great buildings. It is here that we come to a dead stop. " Rien ne va plus." Here we have no Parthenons.

The standard of the house is a question of a practical and constructive order. I have attempted to set it forth in the preceding chapter on airplanes.

The standard of furniture is in its full flood of experiment among the makers of office furniture and trunks, clock-makers and so on. We have only to follow this path : a task for the engineer. And all the humbug talked about the unique object, the precious " piece," rings false and shows a pitiful

CAPRONI-EXPLORATION

Poetry lies not only in the spoken or written word. The poetry of facts is stronger still. Objects which signify something and which are arranged with talent and with tact create a poetic fact.

lack of understanding of the needs of the present day : a chair is in no way a work of art ; a chair has no soul ; it is a machine for sitting in.

Art, in a highly cultivated country, finds its means of expression in pure art, a concentrated thing free from all utilitarian motives—painting, literature, music.

Every human manifestation involves a certain quantum of interest and particularly so in the æsthetic domain ; this interest may be of an order dealing with the senses or of an intellectual order. Decoration is of a sensorial and elementary order, as is colour, and is suited to simple races, peasants and savages. Harmony and proportion incite the intellectual faculties and arrest the man of culture. The peasant loves ornament and decorates his walls. The civilized man wears a well-cut suit and is the owner of easel pictures and books.

Decoration is the essential overplus, the quantum of the peasant ; and proportion is the essential overplus, the quantum of the cultivated man.

In architecture, the quantum of interest is achieved by the grouping and proportion of rooms and furniture ; a task for the architect. And beauty ? This is an imponderable which cannot function except in the actual presence of its primordial bases : the reasonable satisfaction of the mind (utility, economy) ; after that, cubes, spheres, cylinders, cones, etc. (sensorial). Then . . . the imponderable, the relationships which create the imponderable : this is genius, inventive genius, plastic genius, mathematical genius, this capacity for achieving order and unity by measurement and for organizing, in accordance with evident laws, all those things which excite and satisfy our visual senses to the fullest degree.

Then there arise those multifarious sensations, which evoke all that a highly cultivated man may have seen, felt and loved ; which release, by means he cannot escape, vibrations he has already experienced in the drama of life : nature, men, the world.

BELLANGER. SALOON

In this period of science, of strife and drama in which the individual is violently tossed about at every moment, the Parthenon appears to us as a living work, full of grand harmonies. The sum of its inevitable elements gives the measure of the degree of perfection to which man can attain when he is absorbed in a problem definitely stated. The perfection in this case is so much outside the normal, that our apprehension of the Parthenon can only correspond nowadays with a very limited range of sensation, and, unexpectedly enough, with sensations of a mechanical kind ; its correspondence is rather with those huge impressive machines with which we are familiar and which may be considered the most perfect results of our

VOISIN. SPORTS TORPEDO, 1921

It is a simpler matter to form a judgment on the clothes of a well-dressed man than on those of a well-dressed woman, since masculine costume is standardized. It is certain that Phidias was at the side of Ictinos and Kallicrates in building the Parthenon, and that he dominated them, since all the temples of the time were of the same type, and the Parthenon surpasses them all beyond measure.

present-day activities, the only products of our civilization which have really " got there."

Phidias would have loved to have lived in this standardized age. He would have admitted the possibility, nay the certainty of success. His vision would have seen in our epoch the conclusive results of his labours. Before long he would have repeated the experience of the Parthenon.

Architecture is governed by standards. Standards are a matter of logic, analysis and precise study. Standards are based

		Resistance.
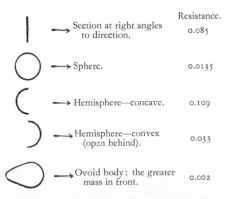	Section at right angles to direction.	0.085
	Sphere.	0.0135
	Hemisphere—concave.	0.109
	Hemisphere—convex (open behind).	0.033
	Ovoid body: the greater mass in front.	0.002

The cone which gives the best penetration is the result of experiment and calculation, and this is confirmed by natural creations such as fishes, birds, etc. Experimental application : the dirigible, racing car.

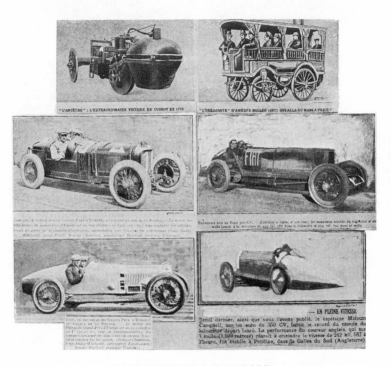

"L'ANCÊTRE": L'EXTRAORDINAIRE VOITURE DE CUGNOT EN 1770

"L'OBÉISSANTE" D'AMÉDÉE BOLLÉE (1873) QUI ALLA DU MANS A PARIS

IN SEARCH OF A STANDARD

THE PARTHENON

Phidias in building the Parthenon did not work as a constructor, engineer or designer. All these elements already existed. What he did was to perfect the work and endue it with a noble spirituality.

on a problem which has been well stated.   Architecture means plastic invention, intellectual speculation, higher mathematics. Architecture is a very noble art.

Standardization is imposed by the law of selection and is an economic and social necessity. Harmony is a state of agreement with the norms of our universe. Beauty governs all ; she is of purely human creation ; she is the overplus necessary only to men of the highest type.

But we must first of all aim at the setting up of standards in order to face the problem of perfection.

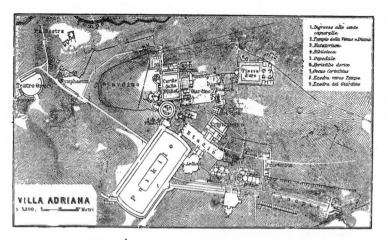

HADRIAN'S VILLA NEAR TIVOLI, 130 A.D.

ARCHITECTURE

I

THE LESSON OF ROME

The business of Architecture is to establish emotional relationships by means of raw materials.

Architecture goes beyond utilitarian needs.

Architecture is a plastic thing.

The spirit of order, a unity of intention.

The sense of relationships ; architecture deals with quantities.

Passion can create drama out of inert stone.

You employ stone, wood and concrete, and with these materials you build houses and palaces. That is construction. Ingenuity is at work.

But suddenly you touch my heart, you do me good, I am happy and I say : " This is beautiful." That is Architecture. Art enters in.

My house is practical. I thank you, as I might thank Railway engineers, or the Telephone service. You have not touched my heart.

But suppose that walls rise towards heaven in such a way that I am moved. I perceive your intentions. Your mood has been gentle, brutal, charming or noble. The stones you have erected tell me so. You fix me to the place and my eyes regard it. They behold something which expresses a thought. A thought which reveals itself without word or sound, but solely by means of shapes which stand in a certain relationship to one another. These shapes are such that they are clearly revealed in light. The relationships between them have not necessarily any reference to what is practical or descriptive. They are a mathematical creation of your mind. They are the language of Architecture. By the use of raw materials and *starting from* conditions more or less utilitarian, you have established certain relationships which have aroused my emotions. This is Architecture.

ROME is a picturesque spot. The sunlight there is so lovely that it excuses everything. Rome is a bazaar where everything is sold. All the utensils of the life of a race have remained there—the child's toy, the soldier's weapons, the ecclesiastical old clothes, the bidets of the Borgias and the adventurer's plumes. In Rome the uglinesses are legion.

If one remembers the Greeks one feels that the Roman had bad taste, the pukka Roman, Julius II and Victor-Emmanuel.

Ancient Rome was packed within walls always too narrow ; a city is not beautiful which is huddled together. Renaissance Rome had its pompous outbursts, spread about in all the corners of the city. The Rome of Victor-Emmanuel garners its legacy, tickets and preserves it, and installs its modern life in the corridors of this museum, and proclaims itself " Roman " by

THE PYRAMID OF CESTIUS, 12 B.C.

the Memorial to Victor-Emmanuel I in the centre of the city between the Capitol and the Forum . . . a work of forty years, something bigger than anything else, and in white marble !

Without doubt everything is too huddled together in Rome.

I

ANCIENT ROME

Rome's business was to conquer the world and govern it. Strategy, recruiting, legislation : the spirit of order. In order to manage a large business house, it is essential to adopt some fundamental, simple and unexceptionable principles. The

THE COLOSSEUM, A.D. 80

THE ARCH OF CONSTANTINE, A.D. 12

INTERIOR OF THE PANTHEON, A.D. 120

Roman order was simple and direct. If it was brutal, so much the worse—or so much the better.

They had enormous desires for domination and organization. Old Rome as regards architecture had nothing to show, the city walls were too crowded, the houses were piled up ten storeys high—the sky-scraper of the ancients. The Forum must have been ugly, a little like the bric-à-brac of the sacred city of Delphi. Town planning, a large lay-out! There was none of this.

Pompeii must be seen, appealing in its rectangular plan. They had conquered Greece and, like good barbarians, they found the Corinthian order more beautiful than the Doric,

THE PANTHEON, A.D. 120

because it was more ornate. On then with the acanthus capitals, and entablatures decorated with little discretion or taste ! But underneath this there was something Roman, as we shall see. Briefly, they constructed superb chassis, but they designed deplorable coachwork rather like the landaus of Louis XIV. Outside Rome, where there was space, they built Hadrian's Villa. One can meditate there on the greatness of Rome. There, they really planned. It is the first example of Western planning on the grand scale. If we cite Greece on this score we may say that " the Greek was a sculptor and nothing more." But wait a little, architecture is not only a question of arrangement. Arrangement is one of the fundamental prerogatives of architecture. To walk in Hadrian's Villa and to have to admit that the modern power of organization (which after all is " Roman ") has done nothing so far —what a torment this is to a man who feels that he is a party to this ingenuous failure !

They did not have before them the problem of devastated regions, but that of equipping conquered regions ; it is all one and the same. So they invented methods of construction and with these they did impressive things—" Roman." The word has a meaning. Unity of operation, a clear aim in view, classification of the various parts. Immense cupolas, with their supporting drums, imposing vaulting, all held together with Roman cement ; these still remain an object of admiration. They were great constructors.

A clear aim, the classification of parts, these are a proof of a special turn of mind : strategy, legislation. Architecture is susceptible to these aims, and repays them with interest. The light plays on pure forms, and repays them with interest. Simple masses develop immense surfaces which display themselves with a characteristic variety according as it is a question of cupolas, vaulting, cylinders, rectangular prisms or pyramids. The adornment of the surfaces is of the same geometrical order. The Pantheon, the Colosseum, the Aqueducts, the Pyramid of Cestius, the Triumphal Arches, the Basilica of Constantine, the Baths of Caracalla.

Absence of verbosity, good arrangement, a single idea,

daring and unity in construction, the use of elementary shapes. A sane morality.

Let us retain, from these Romans, their bricks and their Roman cement and their Travertine and we will sell the Roman marble to the millionaires. The Romans knew nothing of the use of marble.

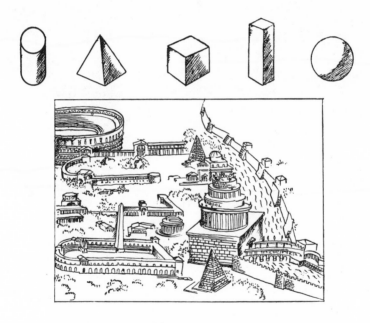

INTERIOR OF S. MARIA IN COSMEDIN

II

BYZANTINE ROME

Renewed impact of Greece, by way of Byzantium. This time it is not the astonishment of a primitive type before the rich entanglement of an acanthus : Greeks by origin come to Rome to build S. Maria in Cosmedin. A Greece very far from Phidias but one which has kept the root of the matter, that is to say the sense of relationships and the mathematical precision thanks to which perfection becomes approachable.

THE NAVE OF S. MARIA IN COSMEDIN, A.D. 790 AND 1120

This quite tiny church of S. Maria, a church for poor people,
set in the midst of noisy and luxurious Rome, proclaims the
noble pomp of mathematics, the unassailable power of proportion, the sovereign eloquence of relationship. The design
is merely that of the ordinary basilica, that is to say the form of
architecture in which barns and hangars are built. The walls
are of rough lime plaster. There is only one colour, white;
always powerful since it is positive. This tiny church commands

THE PULPIT IN S. MARIA IN COSMEDIN

your respect. " Oh ! " you exclaim, coming from St. Peter's
or the Palatine or the Colosseum. The sensualists in art, the
animalists in art would be annoyed by S. Maria in Cosmedin.
To think that this church was in existence in Rome when the
great Renaissance was in full swing with its gilded palaces and
its horrors !

Greece by way of Byzantium, a pure creation of the spirit.
Architecture is nothing but ordered arrangement, noble prisms,

<u>seen in light</u>. There exists one thing which can ravish us, and
this is measure or scale. To achieve scale ! To map out in
rhythmical quantities, animated by an even impulse, to bring
life into the whole by means of a unifying and subtle relationship, to balance, to *resolve the equation*. For, if this expression
may be a paradox in talking of painting, it fits well with
architecture ; with architecture which does not concern
itself with representation or with any element that relates
to the human countenance, with architecture which works
by *quantities*.

These quantities provide a mass of material as a basis for
work ; brought into measure, introduced into the equation,
they result in rhythms, they speak to us of numbers, of relationships, of mind.

In the balanced silence of S. Maria in Cosmedin there stand
out the sloping handrail of a pulpit and the inclined stone
book-rest of an ambo in a conjunction as silent as a gesture
of assent. These two quiet oblique lines which are fused in
the perfect movement of a spiritual mechanics—this is the pure
and simple beauty that architecture can give.

THE APSES OF ST. PETER'S AT ROME

III
MICHAEL ANGELO

Intelligence and passion; there is no art without emotion, no emotion without passion. Stones are dead things sleeping in the quarries but the apses of St. Peter's are a drama. Drama lies all round the key achievements of humanity. The drama of Architecture is the same as that of the man who lives by and through the universe. The Parthenon is moving; the Egyptian Pyramids, of granite once polished and shining like

THE APSES OF ST. PETER'S

steel, were moving. To give forth emanations, storm, gentle breezes on plain and sea, to raise mighty Alps with the pebbles that go to form the walls of men's houses, this is to succeed in a symphony of relationships.

As the man, so the drama, so the architecture. We must not assert with too much conviction that the masses give rise to their man. A *man* is an exceptional phenomenon occurring at long intervals, perhaps by chance, perhaps in accordance with the pulsation of a cosmography not yet understood.

ENTABLATURE OF THE APSES OF ST. PETER'S (MICHAEL ANGELO)

PLAN OF ST. PETER'S AS IT EXISTS

The Nave has been extended as shown by the shading ; Michael Angelo had
something to say ; it has all been destroyed.

Michael Angelo is the man of the last thousand years as Phidias was the man of the thousand years before. The Renaissance did not produce Michael Angelo, it only produced a crowd of talented fellows.

The work of Michael Angelo is a *creation*, not a Renaissance, and overshadows the classical epochs. The apses of St. Peter's are Corinthian. Imagine it ! Look at them and think of the Madeleine. He had seen the Colosseum and retained its rare proportions ; the Thermæ of Caracalla and the Basilica of Con-

PORTA PIA BY MICHAEL ANGELO

stantine showed him the limits which he could expediently
exceed in his high aims. And so we have the rotundas, the
set-backs, the intersecting walls, the drum of the dome, the
hypostyle porch, a gigantic geometry of harmonious relationships. Then we have renewed rhythms in the stylobates,
pilasters, and entablatures of entirely new sections. Then the
windows and niches which begin the rhythm yet once again.
The total mass provides an arresting novelty in the dictionary
of architecture ; it is salutary to stop and reflect for a moment
on this thunderbolt, after the Quintocento.

Finally, St. Peter's should have had an interior which
would have been the monumental climax of a S. Maria in

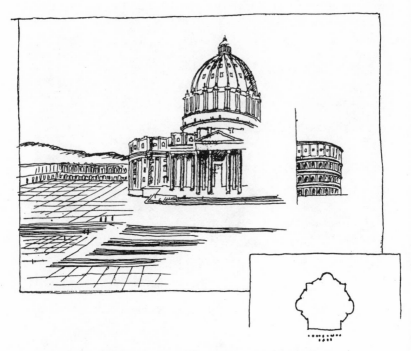

ST. PETER'S. SCHEME BY MICHAEL ANGELO (1547–1564)

The dimensions are considerable. To construct such a dome in stone was a tour de force that few men would have dared. St. Peter's covers an area of about 18,000 square yards as against Notre Dame, about 7,000 square yards, and Sta. Sophia at Constantinople about 8,000. The dome is 404 feet in height; the width across the transepts is 150 yards. The general arrangement of the apses and of the Attic storey is allied to that of the Colosseum; the heights are the same. The whole scheme was a complete unity; it grouped together elements of the noblest and richest kind: the Portico, the cylinders, the square shapes, the drum, the dome. The mouldings are of an intensely passionate character, harsh and pathetic. The whole design would have risen as a single mass, unique and entire. The eye would have taken it in as one thing. Michael Angelo completed the apses and the drum of the dome. The rest fell into barbarian hands; all was spoilt. Mankind lost one of the highest works of human intelligence. If one can imagine Michael Angelo as cognizant of the disaster, we have a terrifying drama.

THE PIAZZA OF ST. PETER'S AS IT IS

Verbose and awkward. Bernini's Colonnade is beautiful in itself. The façade is beautiful in itself, but bears no relation to the Dome. The real aim of the building was the Dome ; it has been hidden ! The Dome was in a proper relation to the apses : they have been hidden. The Portico was a solid mass : it has become merely a front

A WINDOW IN THE APSES OF ST. PETER'S

Cosmedin ; the Medici Chapel at Florence shows on what a scale this work, of which the pattern had been so well established, would have been realized. But foolish and thoughtless Popes dismissed Michael Angelo ; miserable men have murdered St. Peter's within and without. It has become stupidly enough the St. Peter's of to-day, like a very rich and pushing cardinal, lacking . . . *everything*. Immense loss ! A passion, an intelligence beyond normal—this was the Everlasting Yea ; it has become sadly enough a " perhaps," an " apparently," an " it may be," an " I am not sure." Wretched failure !

Since this chapter is entitled *Architecture*, it may be thought excusable to speak therein of the passion of a man.

IV

ROME AND OURSELVES

Rome is a bazaar in full swing, and a picturesque one. There you find every sort of horror (see the four reproductions here given) and the bad taste of the Roman Renaissance. We have to judge this Renaissance by our modern taste, which separates us from it by four great centuries of effort, the 17th, 18th, 19th, and 20th.

We reap the benefit of this endeavour ; we judge hardly, but with a warrantable severity. These four centuries are lacking at Rome, which fell asleep after Michael Angelo. Setting foot once again in Paris, we recover our ability to judge.

The lesson of Rome is for wise men, for those who know and can appreciate, who can resist and can verify. Rome is the damnation of the half-educated. To send architectural students to Rome is to cripple them for life. The Grand Prix de Rome and the Villa Medici are the cancer of French architecture.

THE ROME OF HORRORS

1. *Renaissance Rome. The Castel Saint Angelo.*
2. *Renaissance Rome. The Galleria Colonna*

1. *Modern Rome. The Palazzo di Guistizia.*
2. *Renaissance Rome. The Palazzo Barberini.*

PLAN OF THE CITY OF CARLSRUHE

ARCHITECTURE

II

THE ILLUSION OF PLANS

The Plan proceeds from within to without ; the exterior is the result of an interior. The elements of architecture are light and shade, walls and space.

Arrangement is the gradation of aims, the classification of intentions.

Man looks at the creation of architecture with his eyes, which are 5 feet 6 inches from the ground. One can only consider aims which the eye can appreciate and intentions which take into account architectural elements. If there come into play intentions which do not speak the language of architecture, you arrive at the illusion of plans, you transgress the rules of the Plan through an error in conception, or through a leaning towards empty show.

You employ stone, wood and concrete, and with these materials you build houses and palaces. That is construction. Ingenuity is at work.

But suddenly you touch my heart, you do me good, I am happy and I say : " This is beautiful." That is Architecture. Art enters in.

My house is practical. I thank you, as I might thank Railway engineers, or the Telephone service. You have not touched my heart.

But suppose that walls rise towards heaven in such a way that I am moved. I perceive your intentions. Your mood has been gentle, brutal, charming or noble. The stones you have erected tell me so. You fix me to the place and my eyes regard it. They behold something which expresses a thought. A thought which reveals itself without word or sound, but solely by means of shapes which stand in a certain relationship to one another. These shapes are such that they are clearly revealed in light. The relationships between them have not necessarily any reference to what is practical or descriptive. They are a mathematical creation of your mind. They are the language of Architecture. By the use of inert materials and *starting from* conditions more or less utilitarian, you have established certain relationships which have aroused my emotions. This is Architecture.

TO make a plan is to determine and fix ideas.

It is to have had ideas.

It is so to order these ideas that they become intelligible, capable of execution and communicable. It is essential therefore to exhibit a precise intention, and to have had ideas in order to be able to furnish oneself with an intention. A plan is to some extent a summary like an analytical contents table. In a form so condensed that it seems as clear as crystal and like a geometrical figure, it contains an enormous quantity of ideas and the impulse of an intention.

In a great public institution, the École des Beaux Arts, the principles of good planning have been studied, and then as time has gone by, dogmas have been established, and recipes and tricks. A method of teaching useful enough at the beginning has become a dangerous practice. To represent the inner meaning certain hallowed external signs and aspects have been fixed. The plan, which is really a cluster of ideas and of the intention essential to this cluster of ideas, has become a piece of paper on which black marks for walls and lines for axes play at a sort of mosaic on a decorative panel making graphic representations of star-patterns, creating an optical illusion. The most beautiful star becomes the Grand Prix de Rome. Now, the plan is the generator, " the plan is the determination of everything ; it is an austere abstraction, an algebrization, and cold of aspect." It is a plan of battle. The battle follows and that is the great moment. The battle is composed of the impact of masses in space and the *morale* of the army is the cluster of predetermined ideas and the driving purpose. Without a good plan nothing exists, all is frail and cannot endure, all is poor even under the clutter of the richest decoration.

From the very start the plan implies the methods of construction to be used ; the architect is above all an engineer. But let us keep strictly to architecture, this thing which endures through the ages. Placing myself entirely at this one angle of vision I commence by drawing attention to this vital fact : a plan proceeds *from within to without*, for a house or a palace is an organism comparable to a living being. I shall speak of the architectural *elements* of the interior. I shall pass on to *arrangement*. In considering the effect of buildings in relation to a site, I shall show that here too the *exterior* is always an *interior*. By means of various fundamental elements which will be clearly shown in diagrams, I can demonstrate the illusion of plans, this illusion which kills architecture, ensnares the mind and creates architectural trickery ; this is the fruit of violating undeniable truths, the result of false conceptions or the fruit of vanity.

A PLAN PROCEEDS FROM WITHIN TO WITHOUT

A building is like a soap bubble. This bubble is perfect and harmonious if the breath has been evenly distributed and regulated from the inside. The exterior is the result of an interior.

In Broussa in Asia Minor, at the Green Mosque, you enter by a little doorway of normal human height ; a quite small vestibule produces in you the necessary change of scale so that you may appreciate, as against the dimensions of the street and the spot you come from, the dimensions with which it is intended to impress you. Then you can feel the noble size of the Mosque and your eyes can take its measure. You are in a

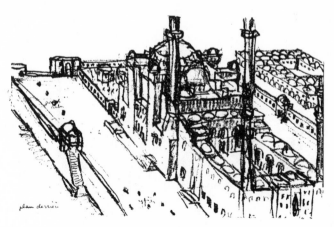

THE SULEIMAN MOSQUE, STAMBOUL

PLAN OF THE GREEN MOSQUE, BROUSSA

great white marble space filled with light. Beyond you can see
a second similar space of the same dimensions, but in half-light
and raised on several steps (repetition in a minor key) ; on
each side a still smaller space in subdued light ; turning round,
you have two very small spaces in shade. From full light to
shade, a rhythm. Tiny doors and enormous bays. You are

SANTA SOPHIA, CONSTANTINOPLE

captured, you have lost the sense of the common scale. You are enthralled by a sensorial rhythm (light and volume) and by an able use of scale and measure, into a world of its own which tells you what it set out to tell you. What emotion, what faith! There you have motive and intention. The cluster of ideas, this is the means that has been used. In con-

THE CASA DEL NOCE.   THE ATRIUM, POMPEII

sequence, at Broussa as at Santa Sophia, as at the Suleiman Mosque of Stamboul, the exterior results from the interior.

CASA DEL NOCE, at Pompeii. Again the little vestibule which frees your mind from the street. And then you are in the Atrium; four columns in the middle (four *cylinders*) shoot up towards the shade of the roof, giving a feeling of force and a witness of potent methods; but at the far end is the brilliance of the garden seen through the peristyle which spreads out this light with a large gesture, distributes it and accentuates it, stretching widely from left to right, making a great space.

Between the two is the Tablium, contracting this vision like the
lens of a camera.   On the right and on the left two patches of
shade—little ones.   Out of the clatter of the swarming street
which is for every man and full of picturesque incident, you
have entered the house of *a Roman*.   Magistral grandeur,
order, a splendid amplitude : you are in the house of *a Roman*.
What was the function of these rooms ?   That is outside the
question.   After twenty centuries, without any historical reference, you are conscious of Architecture, and we are speaking
of what is in reality a very small house.

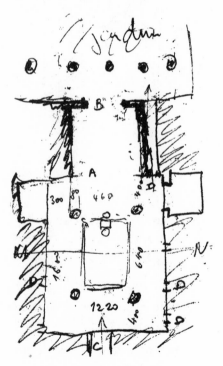

THE CASA DEL NOCE

ARCHITECTURAL ELEMENTS OF THE INTERIOR

Our elements are vertical walls, the spread of the soil, holes to serve as passages for man or for light, doors or windows. The holes give much or little light, make gay or sad. The walls are in full brilliant light, or in half shade or in full shade, giving an effect of gaiety, serenity or sadness. Your symphony is made ready. The aim of architecture is to make you gay or serene. Have respect for walls. The Pompeian did not cut up his wall-spaces ; he was devoted to wall-spaces and loved light. Light is intense when it falls between walls which reflect it.

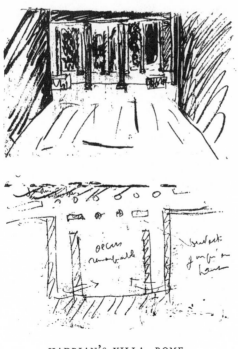

HADRIAN'S VILLA, ROME

The ancients built walls, walls which stretch out and meet to amplify the wall. In this way they created volumes, which are the basis of architectural and sensorial feeling. The light bursts on you, by a definite intention, at one end and illuminates the

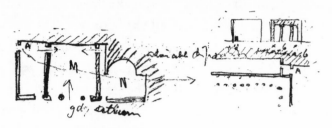

HADRIAN'S VILLA, ROME

walls. The *impression* of light is extended outside by cylinders (I hardly like to say columns, it is a worn-out word), peristyles or pillars. The floor stretches everywhere it can, uniformly and without irregularity. Sometimes, to help the effect, the floor is

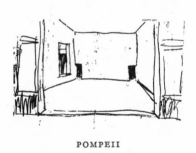

POMPEII

raised by a step. There are no other architectural elements internally : light, and its reflection in a great flood by the walls and the floor, which is really a horizontal wall. To erect well-lit walls is to establish the architectural elements of the interior. There remains to achieve Proportion.

ARRANGEMENT

An axis is perhaps the first human manifestation; it is the means of every human act. The toddling child moves along an axis, the man striving in the tempest of life traces for himself an axis. The axis is the regulator of architecture. To establish order is to begin to work. Architecture is based on axes. The axes of the Schools are an architectural calamity. The axis is a line of direction leading to an end. In architecture, you must have a destination for your axis. In the Schools they have forgotten this and their axes cross one another in star-shapes, all leading to infinity, to the undefined, to the unknown, to nowhere, without end or aim. The axis of the Schools is a recipe and a dodge.

Arrangement is the grading of axes, and so it is the grading of aims, the classification of intentions.

The architect therefore assigns destinations to his axes. These ends are the wall (the plenum, sensorial sensation) or light and space (again sensorial sensation).

In actual fact a birds'-eye view such as is given by a plan on a drawing-board is not how axes are seen; they are seen from the ground, the beholder standing up and looking in front of him. The eye can reach a considerable distance and, like a clear lens, sees everything even beyond what was intended or wished. The axis of the Acropolis runs from the Piræus to Pentelicus, from the sea to the mountain. The Propylea are at right angles to the axis, in the distance on the horizon—the sea.

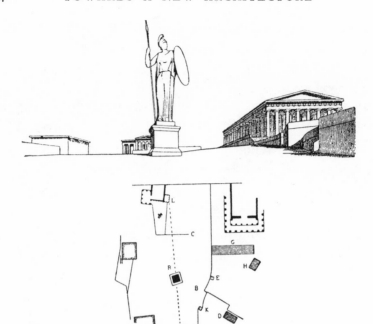

THE ACROPOLIS, ATHENS

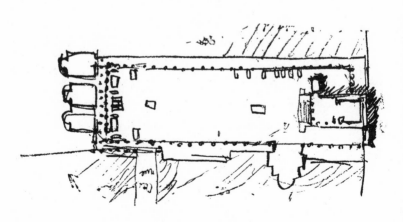

THE FORUM, POMPEII

In the horizontal, at right angles to the direction that the architectural arrangement has impressed on you from where you
stand, it is the rectangular impression which tells. This is architecture of a high order: the Acropolis extends its effect right
to the horizon. The Propylea in the other direction, the colossal
statue of Athena on the axis, and Pentelicus in the distance.
That is what tells. And because they are outside this forceful
axis, the Parthenon to the right and the Erechtheum to the left,
you are enabled to get a three-quarter view of them, in their full
aspects. Architectural buildings should not all be placed upon
axes, for this would be like so many people all talking at once.

THE FORUM OF POMPEII : Arrangement is the grading of
aims, the classification of intentions. The plan of the Forum
contains a number of axes, but it would never obtain even a
bronze medal at the Beaux Arts ; it would be refused, it doesn't
make a star ! It is a joy to the mind to consider such a plan
and to walk in the Forum.

And here IN THE HOUSE OF THE TRAGIC POET we have the
subtleties of a consummate art. Everything is on an axis, but
it would be difficult to apply a true line anywhere. The axis is
in the intention, and the display afforded by the axis extends to
the humbler things which it treats most skilfully (the corridors,
the main passage, etc.) by optical illusions. The axis here is
not an arid thing of theory ; it links together the main volumes
which are clearly stated and differentiated one from another.
When you visit the House of the Tragic Poet, it is clear that
everything is ordered. But the feeling it gives is a rich one.
You then note clever distortions of the axis which give inten-

sity to the volumes : the central motive of the pavement is set behind the middle of the room ; the well at the entrance is at the side of the basin. The fountain at the far end is in the angle of the garden. An object placed in the centre of a room often spoils the room, for it hinders you from standing in the

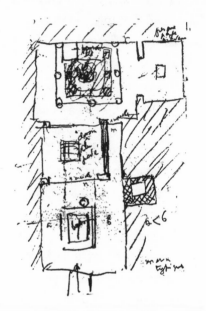

HOUSE OF THE TRAGIC POET, POMPEII

middle of the room and getting the axial view ; a monument placed in the middle of a square often spoils the square and the buildings which surround it—often but not always ; in this matter each case must be judged on its merits.

Arrangement is the grading of axes, and so it is the grading of aims, the classification of intentions.

THE EXTERIOR IS ALWAYS AN INTERIOR

When, at the Schools, they draw axes in the shape of a star, they imagine that the spectator arriving in front of a building is aware of it alone, and that his eye must infallibly follow and remain exclusively fixed on the centre of gravity determined by these axes. The human eye, in its investigations, is always on the move and the beholder himself is always turning right and left, and shifting about. He is interested in everything and is attracted towards the centre of gravity of the whole site. At once the problem spreads to the surroundings. The houses near by, the distant or neighbouring mountains, the horizon low or high, make formidable masses which exercise the force of their cubic volume. This cubic volume, as it appears and as it really is, is instantly gauged and anticipated by the intelligence. This sensation of cubic volume is immediate and fundamental; your building may cube 100,000 cubic yards, but what lies around it may cube millions of cubic yards, and that is what tells. Then there comes in the sensation of density: a tree or a hill is less powerful and of a feebler density than a geometrical disposition of forms. Marble is denser, both to the eye and to the mind, than is wood, and so forth. Always you have gradation.

To sum up, in architectural ensembles, the elements of the site itself come into play by virtue of their cubic volume, their density and the quality of the material of which they are composed, bringing sensations which are very definite and very

THE PROPYLEA AND THE TEMPLE OF THE WINGLESS VICTORY

varied (wood, marble, a tree, grass, blue horizons, near or distant sea, sky). The elements of the site rise up like walls panoplied in the power of their cubic co-efficient, stratification, material, etc., like the walls of a room. Walls in

THE PROPYLEA

relation to light, light and shade, sadness, gaiety or serenity, etc. Our compositions must be formed of these elements.

On the ACROPOLIS AT ATHENS the temples are turned towards one another, making an enclosure, as it were, which the eye readily embraces ; and the sea which composes with the architraves, etc. This is to compose with the infinite resources

HADRIAN'S VILLA, ROME

of an art full of dangerous riches out of which beauty can only come when they are brought into order.

At HADRIAN'S VILLA the levels are established in accordance with the Campagna ; the mountains support the composition, which indeed is based upon them.

In the FORUM OF POMPEII, with its vistas of each building in relation to the whole and to every detail, there is a grouping of varied interest constantly renewed.

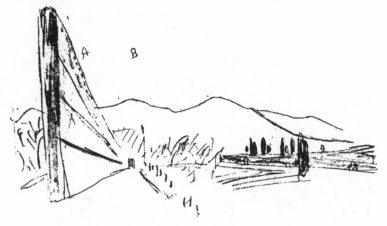

HADRIAN'S VILLA, ROME

THE FORUM, POMPEII

TRANSGRESSION

In the examples I shall now give, the architect has not taken into account that a plan proceeds from within to without, and has not formed his composition out of volumes quickened by a single well-ordered impulse, in conformity with an aim which was the driving intention of the work ; an aim that everyone

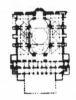

SANTA SOPHIA,
CONSTANTINOPLE

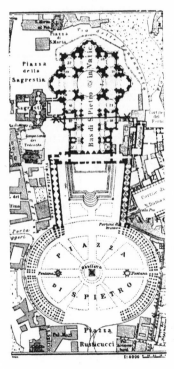

ST. PETER'S, ROME

The line drawn across the third bay of the Nave shows the place where Michael Angelo intended his façade to come (see Michael Angelo's original scheme in the preceding chapter).

could afterwards see for himself with his own eyes. The architect has not taken into account the architectural elements of the interior, that is to say surfaces which are linked together in order to receive light and make manifest the content of the building. He has not thought in terms of space, but has made stars on paper and drawn axes to form these stars. He has dealt with intentions which do not belong to the language of architecture. He has transgressed the rules of proper planning by an error of conception or an inclination towards vanities.

St. Peter's at Rome : Michael Angelo constructed the enormous dome surpassing everything that had been seen till then ; immediately on entering you were under the immense cupola. But the Popes have added three bays in front and a great vestibule. The whole idea is destroyed. Nowadays it is necessary to traverse a tunnel more than 300 feet long before arriving at the dome ; two equivalent masses are in conflict ; the effect of the architecture is lost (and with its decoration, conceitedly coarse, the fundamental fault is enormously increased and St. Peter's remains an enigma for the architect). Santa Sophia at Constantinople is a triumph with its superficial area of about 7,500 square yards, whereas St. Peter's covers an area of more than 16,000.

Versailles : Louis XIV is no longer merely the successor of Louis XIII. He is the Roi-Soleil. Immense vanity ! At the foot of the throne, his architects brought to him plans drawn from a bird's-eye view which seem like a chart of stars ; immense axes, formed like stars. The Roi-Soleil swells with pride ; and gigantic works are carried out. But a man has

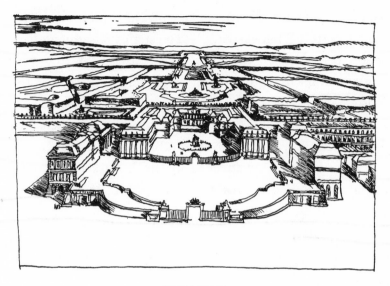

VERSAILLES

(*From a contemporary drawing*)

only two eyes at a level of about 5 feet 6 inches above the ground, and can only look at one point at a time. The arms of the stars are only visible one after the other, and what you have is really a right angle masked by foliation. A right angle is not a star; the stars fall to pieces. And so it goes on : the great basin, the embroidered flower-beds which are outside the general panorama, the buildings that one can only see in fragments and as one moves about. It is a snare and a delusion. Louis XIV deceived himself of his own free will. He transgressed the truths of architecture because he did not work with the objective elements of architecture.

And a little grand-ducal princeling, a courtier, like so many others, of the glory of the Roi-Soleil, planned the town of

CARLSRUHE which is the most lamentable failure of an intention, the perfect " knock-out." [1]   The star exists only on paper, a poor consolation. Illusion ! The illusion of fine plans. From any point in the town you can never see more than three windows of the castle and they always seem the same ones ; the humblest everyday house would produce as much effect. From the castle, you can never look down more than a single street at a time, and any street in any small market town would have a similar effect. Vanity of vanities ! It must not be forgotten, in drawing out a plan, that it is the human eye that judges the result. [2]

When we pass from mere construction to architecture it is because we are indulging a high aim.   Vanity must be avoided. Vanity is the cause of architectural vanities.

[1] I apologize for the retention here of the original *French*.—F. E.
[2] See the Plan of Carlsruhe at the head of this Section.

THE PARTHENON

ARCHITECTURE

III

PURE CREATION OF THE MIND

Profile and contour are the touchstone of the Architect.

Here he reveals himself as artist or mere engineer.

Profile and contour are free of all constraint.

There is here no longer any question of custom, nor of tradition, nor of construction, nor of adaptation to utilitarian needs.

Profile and contour are a pure creation of the mind ; they call for the plastic artist.

You employ stone, wood and concrete, and with these materials you build houses and palaces; that is construction. Ingenuity is at work.

But suddenly you touch my heart, you do me good, I am happy and I say : " This is beautiful." That is Architecture. Art enters in.

My house is practical. I thank you, as I might thank Railway engineers or the Telephone service. You have not touched my heart.

But suppose that walls rise towards heaven in such a way that I am moved. I perceive your intentions. Your mood has been gentle, brutal, charming or noble. The stones you have erected tell me so. You fix me to the place and my eyes regard it. They behold something which expresses a thought. A thought which reveals itself without word or sound, but solely by means of shapes which stand in a certain relationship to one another. These shapes are such that they are clearly revealed in light. The relationships between them have not necessarily any reference to what is practical or descriptive. They are a mathematical creation of your mind. They are the language of Architecture. By the use of inert materials and *starting from* conditions more or less utilitarian, you have established certain relationships which have aroused my emotions. This is Architecture.

THE distinction of a fine face lies in the quality of the features and in a quite special and personal value of the relationship between them. The same general type of face is the property of every individual : nose, mouth, forehead, etc., and also the same general proportion between these elements. There are millions of countenances constructed on these essential lines ; nevertheless all are different : there is a variation in the quality of the features and in the relationship which unites them. We say that a face is handsome when the precision of the modelling and the disposition of the features reveal proportions which we *feel to be harmonious* because they arouse, deep within us and beyond our senses, a resonance, a sort of sounding-board which begins to vibrate. An indefinable trace of the Absolute which lies in the depths of our being.

THE PARTHENON

The Greeks on the Acropolis set up temples which are animated by a single thought, drawing around them the desolate landscape and gathering it into the composition. *Thus, on every point of the horizon, the thought is single. It is on this account that there are no other architectural works on this scale of grandeur. We shall be able to talk " Doric " when man, in nobility of aim and complete sacrifice of all that is accidental in Art, has reached the higher levels of the mind : austerity.*

INTERNAL PORTICO OF THE PROPYLEA

The Plastic scheme is expressed in unity.

188

THE PROPYLEA

From what is emotion born? From a certain relationship between definite elements : cylinders, an even floor, even walls. From a certain harmony with the things that make up the site. From a plastic system that spreads its effects over every part of the composition. From a unity of idea that reaches from the unity of the materials used to the unity of the general contour.

THE PROPYLEA

Emotion is born of unity of aim; of that unperturbed resolution that wrought its marble with the firm intention of achieving all that is most pure, most clarified, most economical. Every sacrifice, every cleansing had already been performed. The moment was reached when nothing more might be taken away, when nothing would be left but these close-knit and violent elements, sounding clear and tragic like brazen trumpets.

THE ERECHTHEUM

There was a breath of tenderness and Ionic was born; but the Parthenon dictated their forms to the Caryatides.

THE PARTHENON

Certain writers have declared that the Doric column was inspired by a tree springing from the earth, without base, etc., a proof that every noble form of art derives from nature. It is most false, since the tree with straight trunk is unknown in Greece, where only stunted pines and twisted olives grow. The Greeks created a plastic system directly and forcibly affecting our senses : *columns and their flutings, a complex entablature rich in meaning ; steps which set off and link on to the horizon. They employed the most delicate distortions, applying to their contours an impeccable adjustment to the laws of optics.*

This sounding-board which vibrates in us is our criterion of harmony. This is indeed the axis on which man is organized in perfect accord with nature and probably with the universe, this axis of organization which must indeed be that on which all phenomena and all objects of nature are based ; this axis leads us to assume a unity of conduct in the universe and to

THE PARTHENON

We must realize clearly that Doric architecture did not grow in the fields with the asphodels, and that it is a pure creation of the mind. The plastic system of Doric work is so pure that it gives almost the feeling of a natural growth. But, none the less, it is entirely man's creation, and affords us the complete sensation of a profound harmony. The forms used are so separate from natural aspect (and how superior they are to those of Egyptian or Gothic architecture), they are so deeply thought out in regard to light and materials, that they seem, as it were, linked to earth and sky, as if by nature. This creates a fact as reasonable to our understanding as the fact " sea " or the fact " mountain." How many works of man have attained this height ?

admit a single will behind it. The laws of physics are thus a corollary to this axis, and if we recognize (and love) science and its works, it is because both one and the other force us to admit that they are prescribed by this primal will. If the results of mathematical calculation appear satisfying and harmonious to us, it is because they proceed from the axis. If, through

THE PARTHENON

The plastic system

THE PARTHENON

Here is something to arouse emotion. We are in the inexorable realm of the mechanical. There are no symbols attached to these forms : they provoke definite sensations ; there is no need of a key in order to understand them. Brutality, intensity, the utmost sweetness, delicacy and great strength. And who discovered the combination of these elements ? An inventor of genius. These stones lay inert in the quarries of Pentelicus, unshaped. To group them thus needed not an engineer, but a great sculptor.

calculation, the airplane takes on the aspect of a fish or some object of nature, it is because it has recovered the axis. If the canoe, the musical instrument, the turbine, all results of experiment and calculation, appear to us to be " organized " phenomena, that is to say as having in themselves a certain life, it is because they are based upon that axis. From this we get a possible definition of harmony, that is to say a moment of accord with the axis which lies in man, and so with the laws of the universe,—a return to universal law. This would afford an explanation of the cause of the satisfaction we experience at the sight of certain objects, a satisfaction which commands at every moment an effective unanimity.

   If we are brought up short by the Parthenon, it is because a chord inside us is struck when we see it ; the axis is touched. We do not stop short in front of the Madeleine, which is made up, just like the Parthenon, of steps, columns and pediments (the same primary elements). And the reason is that behind and beyond the grosser sensations, the Madeleine cannot touch our axis ; we do not feel the profounder harmonies, and are not rooted to the spot by the recognition of these.

   The objects in nature and the results of calculation are clearly and cleanly formed ; they are organized without ambiguity. It is because *we see clearly* that we can read, learn and feel their harmony. I repeat : *clear statement* is essential in a work of art.

   If the works of nature *live*, and if the creations of calculation

THE PROPYLEA

Everything is stated exactly, the mouldings are tight and firm, relationships are established between the annulets of the capital, the abacus and the bands of the architrave.

move and produce activity in us, it is because they are both animated by a unity of the intention which is responsible for them. I repeat : there must be a unity of aim in the work of art.

If the objects of nature and if the creations of calculation gain our attention and awaken our interest, it is because both one and the other have a fundamental attitude which characterizes them. I repeat : a work of art must have its own special character.

THE PARTHENON

The fraction of the inch comes into play. The curve of the echinus is as rational as that of a large shell. The annulets are 50 feet from the ground, but they tell more than all the baskets of acanthus on a Corinthian capital. The Doric state of mind and the Corinthian state of mind are two things. A moral fact creates a gulf between them.

Clear statement, the giving of a living unity to the work, the giving it a fundamental attitude and a character : all this is a pure creation of the mind.

This is everywhere allowed in the case of painting and music ; but architecture is lowered to the level of its utilitarian purposes : boudoirs, W.C.'s, radiators, ferro-concrete, vaults or pointed arches, etc., etc. This is construction,

FROM A MAGNIFICENT PLASTER CAST AT THE BEAUX-ARTS

this is not architecture. Architecture only exists when there is a poetic emotion. Architecture is a plastic thing. I mean by "plastic" what is seen and measured by the eyes. Obviously, if the roof were to fall in, if the central heating did not work, if the walls cracked, the joys of architecture would be greatly diminished ; the same thing might be said of a gentleman who listened to a symphony sitting on a pin-cushion or in a bad draught.

Almost every period of architecture has been linked on to research into construction. The conclusion has often been

THE PARTHENON

The fraction of the inch comes into play. The mouldings contain a number of elements, but everything is ordered with a view to strength. Astonishing distortions : the bands are incurved or bend over outwards in order to display themselves better to the eye. Incised lines, in half shade, form an edge to shadows which would otherwise be vague.

drawn that architecture is construction. It may be that the effort put forth by architects has been mainly concentrated on the constructional problems of the time ; that is not a reason for mixing different things. It is quite true that the architect should have construction as least as much at his fingers' ends as a thinker his grammar. And construction being a much

THE PARTHENON

All this plastic machinery is realized in marble with the rigour that we have learned to apply in the machine. The impression is of naked polished steel.

more difficult and complex science than grammar, an architect's efforts are concentrated on it for a large part of his career; but he should not vegetate there.

The plan of the house, its cubic mass and its surfaces have been dictated partly by the utilitarian demands of the problem,

Q

and partly by imagination, *i.e.*, plastic creation. Here at once, in regard to the plan and consequently in regard to whatever is erected in space, the architect has worked plastically; he has restrained utilitarian demands in deference to the plastic aim he was pursuing; *he has made a composition.*

Then comes the moment when he must carve the *lineaments of the outward aspect.* He has brought the play of light and shade to the support of what he wanted to say. Profile and contour have entered in, and they are free of all constraint; they are a pure invention which makes the outward aspect radiant or dulls it. It is in his contours that we can trace the plastic artist; the engineer is effaced and the sculptor comes to life. Contours are the touchstone of the architect; in dealing with them he is forced to decide whether he will be a plastic artist or not. Architecture is the skilful, accurate and magnificent play of masses seen in light; and contours are also and exclusively the skilful, accurate and magnificent play of volumes seen in light. Contours go beyond the scope of the practical man, the daring man, the ingenious man; they call for the plastic artist.

Greece, and in Greece the Parthenon, have marked the apogee of this pure creation of the mind: the development of profile and contour.

We can see that it is no longer a question of customary use nor of tradition, nor of constructional methods, nor of adaptation to utilitarian needs. It is a question of pure invention, so personal that it may be called that of one man; Phidias made the Parthenon, for Ictinus and Callicrates, the official architects of the Parthenon, built other Doric temples which seem to us cold and not over-interesting. Passion, generosity and magnanimity are so many virtues written into the geometry of

THE PARTHENON
Austere profiles.   Doric morality.

the handling of the contour,—volumes disposed in precise relationships.   Phidias, Phidias the great sculptor, made the Parthenon.

There has been nothing like it anywhere or at any period.

It happened at a moment when things were at their keenest, when a man, stirred by the noblest thoughts, crystallized them in a plastic work of light and shade. The mouldings of the Parthenon are infallible and implacable. In severity they go far beyond our practice, or man's normal capabilities. Here,

THE PARTHENON
The audacity of square mouldings

the purest witness to the physiology of sensation, and to the mathematical speculation attached to it, is fixed and determined : we are riveted by our senses ; we are ravished in our minds ; we touch the axis of harmony. No question of religious dogma enters in ; no symbolical description, no naturalistic representation ; there is nothing but pure forms in precise relationships.

For two thousand years, those who have seen the Parthenon have felt that here was a decisive moment in Architecture.

We are at a decisive moment. At the present time when the arts are feeling their way and when painting, for instance, is

THE PARTHENON

The audacity of the square mouldings ; austerity and nobility.

finding little by little the formulas of a healthy mode of expression and so jars violently on the spectator, the Parthenon gives us sure truths and emotion of a superior, mathematical order. Art is poetry : the emotion of the senses, the joy of the mind as it measures and appreciates, the recognition of an axial principle which touches the depth of our being. Art is this

pure creation of the spirit which shows us, at certain heights, the summit of the *creation* to which man is capable of attaining. And man is conscious of great happiness when he *feels that he is creating*.

THE PARTHENON

The tympanum of the pediment is bare. The section of the cornice is as tight as an engineer's outline.

MASS-PRODUCTION
HOUSES

A great epoch has begun.

There exists a new spirit.

Industry, overwhelming us like a flood which rolls on towards its destined end, has furnished us with new tools adapted to this new epoch, animated by the new spirit.

Economic law unavoidably governs our acts and our thoughts.

The problem of the house is a problem of the epoch. The equilibrium of society to-day depends upon it. Architecture has for its first duty, in this period of renewal, that of bringing about a revision of values, a revision of the constituent elements of the house.

Mass-production is based on analysis and experiment.

Industry on the grand scale must occupy itself with building and establish the elements of the house on a mass-production basis.

We must create the mass-production spirit.

The spirit of constructing mass-production houses.

The spirit of living in mass-production houses.

The spirit of conceiving mass-production houses.

If we eliminate from our hearts and minds all dead concepts in regard to the houses and look at the question from a critical and objective point of view, we shall arrive at the " House-Machine," the mass-production house, healthy (and morally so too) and beautiful in the same way that the working tools and instruments which accompany our existence are beautiful.

Beautiful also with all the animation that the artist's sensibility can add to severe and pure functioning elements.

THE programme demanded in France by MM. Loucheur and Bonnevay was for a law authorizing the construction of 500,000 dwellings to be built well and cheaply. This was an exceptional event in the annals of construction and required exceptional means and methods.

Now, it was necessary to start from the very beginning; nothing being ready for the realization of such an immense programme. *The right state of mind does not exist.*

The state of mind for mass-production houses, the state of mind for living in mass-production houses, the state of mind for conceiving mass-production houses.

Everything must be begun from the beginning, nothing is ready. Specialization has hardly touched the domain of the dwelling-house. There are neither the workshops nor the technical specialists.

But at any moment, if once the mass-production spirit came to life, everything would quickly be begun. In fact, in every branch of building, Industry, as formidable as a natural force and overrunning everything like a flood that rolls on to its destined end, tends more and more to transform natural raw materials and to produce what we call " new materials." They are legion : cements and limes, steel girders, sanitary fittings, insulating materials, piping, ironmongery, water-proofing compositions, etc., etc. All this stuff is dumped in bulk into buildings in course of construction, and is worked into the job on the spot ; this involves enormous costs in labour and leads

LE CORBUSIER, 1915. A GROUP OF MASS-PRO⟨

The walls and partitions were a light filling of bricks, breeze slabs and so on, cap-
able of being erected by unskilled labour. The height of two slabs was arranged to
agree with that of the doors, cupboards and windows, which were all worked to one
unit of measurement. Contrary to normal practice, the woodwork (mass-produced)

LE CORBUSIER, 1920

The concrete was poured in from above as you would fill a bottle. A house can ⟨
completed in three days. It comes out from the shuttering like a casting. But th⟨
shocks our contemporary architects, who cannot believe in a house that is made ⟨

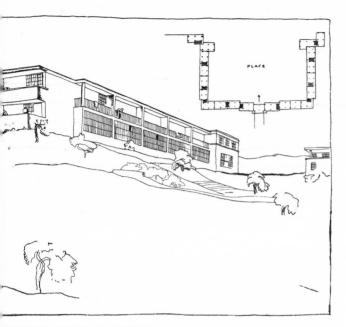

DUCTION HOUSES IN REINFORCED CONCRETE

was fixed before the walls, and so dictated the alignment both of these and of the internal partitions ; both walls and partitions were worked round the woodwork, and the houses were thus completed by a single body of workmen : masons.   All that remained was to install the pipes for the various services.

CONCRETE HOUSES

three days ; we must take a year to build it, and we must have pointed roofs, dormers and mansards.

to half-and-half solutions. The reason is that the various objects have not been standardized. As the necessary state of mind does not exist, attention has never been given to the serious study of the various units, and still less to that of the construction itself; the mass-production state of mind is hateful to architects and to the ordinary man (by infection and persuasion).

The prime consequences of the industrial evolution in " building " show themselves in this first stage ; the replacing of natural materials by artificial ones, of heterogeneous and doubtful materials by homogeneous and artificial ones (tried and proved in the laboratory) and by products of fixed composition. Natural materials, which are infinitely variable in composition, must be replaced by fixed ones.

On the other hand the laws of Economics demand their rights : steel girders and, more recently, reinforced concrete, are pure manifestations of calculation, using the material of which they are composed in its entirety and absolutely exactly ; whereas in the old-world timber beam there may be lurking some treacherous knot, and the very way in which it is squared up means a heavy loss in material.

Lastly, in certain fields, the technical experts have already spoken. Water supply and lighting services are rapidly being evolved ; central heating has begun to take into consideration the structure of walls and windows—surfaces which tend to cooling, for instance—and in consequence stone, the good old material stone, used for walls 3 feet thick or more, is seen to be more than outmatched by light cavity walls in breeze slabs, and so on. Accepted things so far treated as almost unassailable no longer hold their own : roofs which need no longer be pointed for purposes of throwing off water, the enormous and handsome window-embrasures which annoy us since they imprison the light and deprive us of it ; the massive timbers, as thick as you please and heavy for all eternity, but which will still spring and split if placed near a radiator, whilst a patent board $\frac{1}{8}$ inch thick will remain intact. . . .

It was a common thing in the good old days (which still go on, alas !) to see heavy horses drawing enormous stones to the yard, and a mass of human labour unloading them, cutting and dressing them, hoisting them on to the scaffolding, placing them in position and, rule in hand, making lengthy adjustments to every face ; such buildings might take two years to construct : to-day a building can be erected in a few months ; the P.O. have recently finished their immense Cold Storage building at Tolbiac. The materials used are confined to grains of sand and coke-breeze the size of small nuts ; the walls are thin like membranes ; but enormous consignments are stored in this building. Thin walls to give protection against differences of temperature, and partitions 3 to 4 inches thick in spite of the enormous loads stored there. Things have indeed altered !

The difficulties of transport are at their height : it is clear that houses represent an immense tonnage. If this were reduced four-fifths, that would indeed be up-to-date ! The war has shaken us all up. Contractors have bought new plant, ingenious, patient and rapid. Will the yard soon be a factory ? There is talk of houses made in a mould by pouring in liquid

N3

LE CORBUSIER, 1915. HOUSE

The constructional method is here applied to a middle-class house, at the same rate per foot cube as a simple workman's house. The architectural resources of the method employed permit of a large and rhythmical arrangement and make

concrete from above, completed in one day as you would fill a bottle.

One thing leads to another, and as so many cannons, airplanes, lorries and wagons had been made in factories, someone asked the question: "Why not make houses?" There you have a state of mind really belonging to our epoch. Nothing is

REINFORCED CONCRETE

real architectural treatment possible. It is here that the mass-production
principle shows its true value : some sort of link between the rich man's house
and the poor man's ; and some sort of decency in the rich man's dwelling.

ready, but everything can be done. In the next twenty years,
big industry will have co-ordinated its standardized materials,
comparable with those of metallurgy ; technical achievement
will have carried heating and lighting and methods of rational
construction far beyond anything we are acquainted with.
Contractors' yards will no longer be sporadic dumps in which

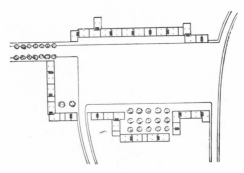

PLAN OF HOUSING SCHEME IN REINFORCED CONCRETE

everything breathes confusion; financial and social organization, using concerted and forceful methods, will be able to solve the housing question, and the yards will be on a huge scale, run and exploited like government offices. Dwellings, urban and suburban, will be enormous and square-built and no longer a dismal congeries; they will incorporate the principle of mass-production and of large-scale industrialization. It is even

HOUSE IN REINFORCED CONCRETE.   HOUSE AND WORKSHOP
The walls do not carry any weight ; the windows go right round the house.

LE CORBUSIER, 1915. INTERIOR OF A REINFORCED CONCRETE HOUSE

Mass-production doors, windows, cupboards : the windows are built up of one, two, a dozen units : one door with one impost, two doors with two imposts, or two doors without impost, etc. ; cupboards glazed above and with drawers below for books, utensils, etc. All these units, which big industry can supply, are based on a common unit of measurement : they can be adapted to one another exactly. The framework of the house being made, these elements are set up in their proper places in the empty shell and temporarily fixed by laths ; the voids are filled by plaster slabs, bricks or lathing ; the normal method of building is reversed and months of work are saved. A further gain, of the greatest importance, is architectural unity, and by means of the module, or unit of measurement, good proportion is assured automatically.

possible that building " to measure " will cease. An inevitable social evolution will have transformed the relationship between tenant and landlord, will have modified the current conception of the dwelling-house, and our towns will be ordered instead of being chaotic. A house will no longer be this solidly-built thing which sets out to defy time and decay, and which is an expensive luxury by which wealth can be shown ; it will be a tool as the motor-car is becoming a tool. The house will no

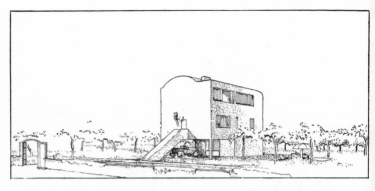

LE CORBUSIER, 1922. ARTIST'S HOUSE

Framework of reinforced concrete with cavity walls, each thickness being about
1½". State your problem clearly to yourself: determine the type of house
according to the needs required; resolve the problem as those of railway
carriages, tools, etc. are resolved.

LE CORBUSIER, 1919.

The ground consisted of layers of gravel. A quarry was opened on the site;
and the gravel was run with lime into a raft 12 inches in thickness; the
floors were in reinforced concrete. An æsthetic of its own results from the
method employed, and to use the resources of the modern industrial "yard" to

LE CORBUSIER, 1922.   MASS-PRODUCTION WORKMEN'S HOUSES

A sensible housing scheme ; the same house-unit being used in varied ways. Four concrete piers ; " cement-gun " walls.   Its æsthetic ?   Architecture is a plastic, not a romantic, affair.

HOUSES OF COARSE CONCRETE

advantage demands the exclusive employment of straight lines, square-set ; this is the grand acquisition of modern architecture, and it is a great gain. We must clear our minds of romantic cobwebs.

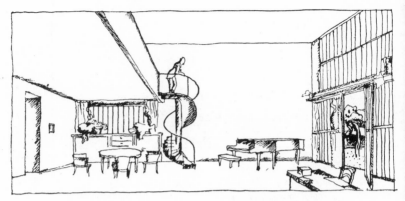

LE CORBUSIER, 1921. MASS-PRODUCTION HOUSE

"*Citrohan*" (*not to say Citroën*). *That is to say, a house like a motor-car, conceived and carried out like an omnibus or a ship's cabin. The actual needs of the dwelling can be formulated and demand their solution. We must fight against the old-world house, which made a bad use of space. We must look upon the house as a machine for living in or as a tool. When a man starts any particular industry he buys the necessary equipment of tools ; when he sets up house he rents, in actual fact, a ridiculous dwelling. Till now a house has consisted of an incoherent grouping of a number of large rooms ; in these rooms the space has been both cramped and wasted. To-day, happily, we are not rich enough to carry on these customs, and as it is difficult to get people to look at the problem under its true aspect (machines for living in), it is nearly impossible to build in our towns, with disastrous results. Windows and doors must have their sizes readjusted ; railway carriages and saloon-cars have shown that man can pass through smaller openings, and that these can be worked out to the last square inch ; it is criminal to make W.C.'s 36 feet square. As the price of building has quadrupled itself, we must reduce the old architectural*

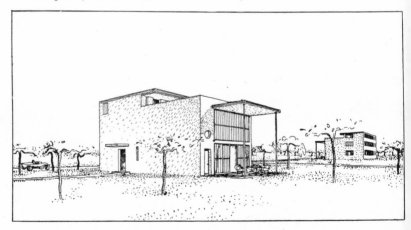

LE CORBUSIER, 1922. MASS-PRODUCTION VILLA

Framework of concrete. A large living-room 30 feet × 16 feet ; kitchen, maids' room ; bedroom, bathroom, boudoir ; two bedrooms and a " solarium."

*pretensions and the cubage of houses by at least one-half; henceforth the pro-
blem is in the hands of the technical expert: we must enlist the discoveries
made in industry and change our attitude altogether.*

As to beauty, this is always present when you have proportion; *and proportion costs the landlord nothing, it is at the charge of the architect! The
emotions will not be aroused unless reason is first satisfied, and this comes
when calculation is employed. There is no shame in living in a house without
a pointed roof, with walls as smooth as sheet iron, with windows like those
of factories. And one* can *be proud of having a house as serviceable as a typewriter.*

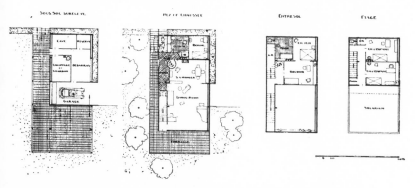

LE CORBUSIER, 1921. A "CITROHAN" HOUSE

*Framework of concrete, girders made on the site and raised by a hand-winch.
Hollow walls of $1\frac{1}{8}''$ concrete and expanded metal with a $7\frac{1}{2}''$ cavity; all floor
slabs on the same unit of measurement; the factory-window frames, with
adaptable ventilating, on the same unit. The arrangements in conformity
with the running of a household; abundant lighting, all hygienic needs met and
servants well cared for.*

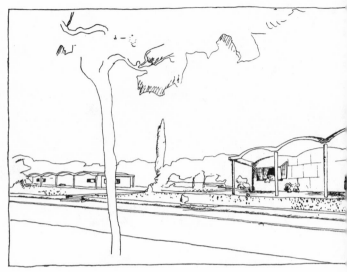

LE CORBUSIER, 1919.

The ordinary house weighs too much and involves the cost of transportation of a quantity of material—bricks, woodwork, cement, tiles, timber, etc. The factory-made house is needed. The constructional principle is that of casings of asbestos sheeting about ¼″ thick, forming courses about 3 feet in height, filled in with rough material, aggregate, rough rubble, etc., found on the site, lightly bound with lime mortar, leaving between them cavities which give the

LE CORBUSIER.

When one talks of mass-production houses one means, of course, the " housing scheme." Unity in the constructional elements is a guarantee of beauty. A housing scheme affords the variety necessary for architectural composition and lends itself to design on a large scale and to real architectural rhythms. A well-mapped-out scheme, constructed on a mass-production basis, can give a feeling

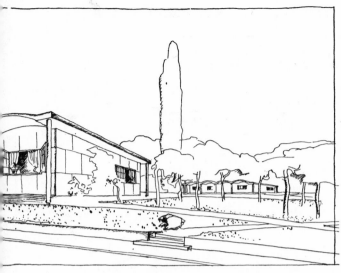

A "MONOL" HOUSE

walls an important insulating quality ; ceilings and floors of arched corrugated asbestos sheets which form a shuttering and receive a coating of concrete an inch or so thick. The corrugated sheets remain permanently and form a definitely insulating layer. The woodwork, windows and doors are adjusted at the same time as the casings. The house is completed by one class of labour, and the only transport needed is that of a double shell of ¼" asbestos sheeting.

A "MONOL" BUILDING

of calm, order and neatness, and inevitably imposes discipline on the inhabitants. America has given us an example by the elimination of hedges and fences, rendered possible only by the modern feeling of respect for other people's property which took its rise over there ; such suburbs give a great sense of space ; for once hedges and fences are removed, light and sunshine reign over all.

LE CORBUSIER, 1921.   A SEASIDE VILLA CONSTRUCTED WITH
MASS-PRODUCTION UNITS

*Reinforced concrete piers every 16 feet in each direction; slightly vaulted
ceilings of reinforced slabs.   Within this framework, which is exactly like
that of industrial buildings, the plan is arranged as required by means of
slender partitions.   The net cost is extremely low.*

*On the æsthetic side there is a gain of the utmost importance in the use of
standard units of dimension.   The lower cost of such a building, as compared
with that of a more complicated form of construction, enables a greater ground
area to be covered with a larger building.   The lightly constructed walls and
partitions can be rearranged at any time and the plan altered at will.*

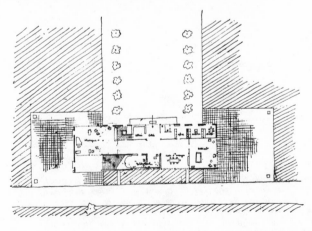

PLAN OF THE VILLA, SHOWING THE PIERS REGULARLY DISPOSED

INTERIOR OF THE SEASIDE VILLA

The concrete piers of uniform section, the flat vaults of the ceilings, the standard-ized window-units, the solids and the voids make up the architectural elements of the construction.

LE CORBUSIER. INTERIOR OF A "MONOL" HOUSE, ARRANGED AS A
MIDDLE-CLASS HOME

If cultivated people realized that mass-construction houses can be built of perfect design and proportion, and at less cost than their flat in town, they would at once insist on a better suburban train service, so that a real use might be made of the city's surrounding country-side.

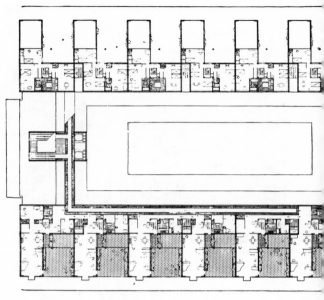

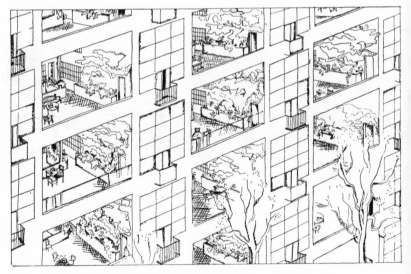

"FREEHOLD MAISONETTES": THE HANGING GARDENS
Each garden is completely shut off from its neighbour.

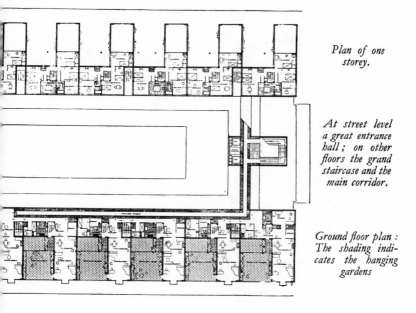

Plan of one storey.

At street level a great entrance hall; on other floors the grand staircase and the main corridor.

Ground floor plan: The shading indicates the hanging gardens

LE CORBUSIER, 1922. A GREAT RENT-PURCHASE SCHEME

The drawings show the arrangement of a group of 100 maisonettes disposed in five storeys, each maisonette having two floors and its own garden. A communal service provides for all necessities and provides the solution to the servant question (which is only just beginning and is an inevitable social fact). Modern achievement, applied to so important an enterprise, replaces human labour by the machine and by good organization; constant hot water, central-heating,

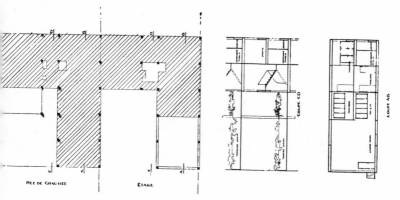

"FREEHOLD MAISONETTES"
Mass-production construction of concrete piers and slabs. Cavity walls.

"FREEHOLD MAISONETTES"

One of the hanging gardens.

refrigerators, vacuum cleaners, pure water, etc. Servants are no longer of necessity tied to the house; they come here, as they would to a factory, and do their eight hours; in this way an active staff is available day and night. The provision of food, whether cooked or not, is arranged by a special purchasing service, which makes for quality and economy. From a vast kitchen the food

"FREEHOLD MAISONETTES"

View of a dining-room (the hanging garden is seen through the window on the right).

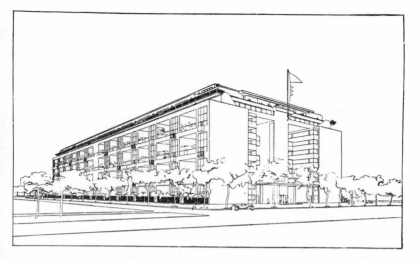

"FREEHOLD MAISONETTES"

General view of one block

is supplied as required to be eaten, either privately or in the communal restaurant. Each maisonette has its own gymnasium and sports room, but on the roof there is a communal hall for sports and a 300 yards track. On the roof too is an entertainment hall for the use of the inhabitants. The ordinary narrow entrance lobby of the house is replaced by a vast hall, and a porter is on duty day and night to receive visitors and show them to the lifts. There is the great covered court, on the roof of the underground garages, for tennis. Trees and flowers all around this court, and all along the street in the gardens; in each hanging garden flowers and creepers. "Standardization" here comes into its own. The maisonettes represent a type of house-arrangement which is rational and sensible, without emphasis in any particular direction, but sufficient and practical. By the system of rent purchase the bad old property systems no longer exist.

No actual rent is paid; the tenants take shares in the enterprise; these are payable over a period of twenty years, and the interest represents a very low rent.

Mass-production is even more essential than anywhere else in great enterprises of this kind: low cost. And the mass-production spirit brings with it many unhoped-for benefits at a difficult time: domestic economy.

"FREEHOLD MAISONETTES": ENTRANCE HALL

If we analyse the 400 square yards allotted to each inhabitant of a garden city, we find that the house and its outbuildings take up 50 to 100 square yards; and 300 square yards are given up to lawns, fruit and vegetable gardens, flower-beds, etc. All this involves an absorbing, costly and laborious upkeep. The result is often a few bunches of carrots and a basket of pears. There is no space left for games or sports. Now it ought to be possible to indulge in games and sports generally at any time on any day right at one's door, not in "sports grounds", which are really only suitable for professionals or people of leisure. Let us put the problem more logically; house 50 square yards with small pleasure garden 50 square yards (both garden and house may be on the ground-floor level or at the sixth storey arranged in "honeycomb" fashion). Around the blocks of flats or maisonnettes large playgrounds for football, tennis, etc., to the tune of 150 square yards per house. In front of the houses a similar area of ground

NEW DWELLINGS AT BORDEAUX

A first group in course of construction

PIERRE JEANNERET, 1925

devoted to agriculture of an industrialized and intensive kind, giving a large yield (irrigation, farmed-out labour, small trucks for moving manure, soil, produce, etc.). A farmer acts as superintendent and manager of a grouping. The agricultural labourer is deserting the country-side; with three shifts of eight hours each in operation, the artisan here becomes his own agricultural labourer and produces an important part of the food he consumes. Architecture? Town planning? The logical study of the cell and its functions in relation to the mass may furnish a solution rich in results.

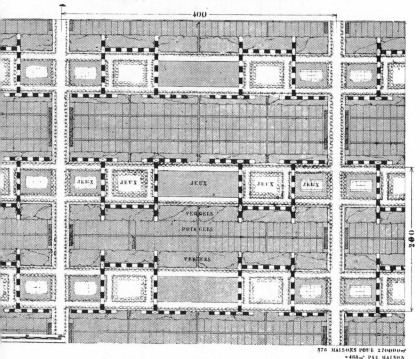

576 MAISONS POUR 270000m²
= 468m² PAR MAISON

OUSING SCHEME FOR GARDEN CITIES ON THE "HONEYCOMB" PRINCIPLE

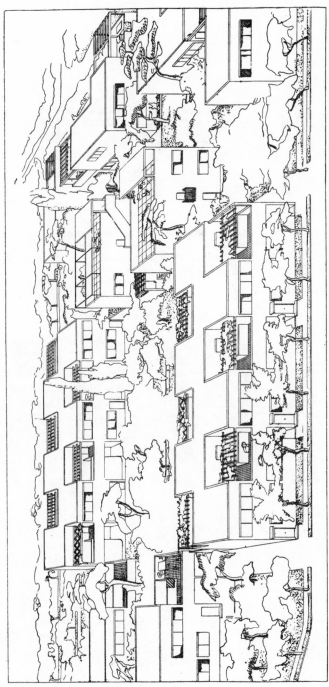

BORDEAUX-PESSAC, 1924. MODERN DWELLINGS

Showing part of a large housing-scheme. The primary elements have been minutely fixed and are multiplied with endless variations. This is a genuine industrialization of the Builders' Yard.

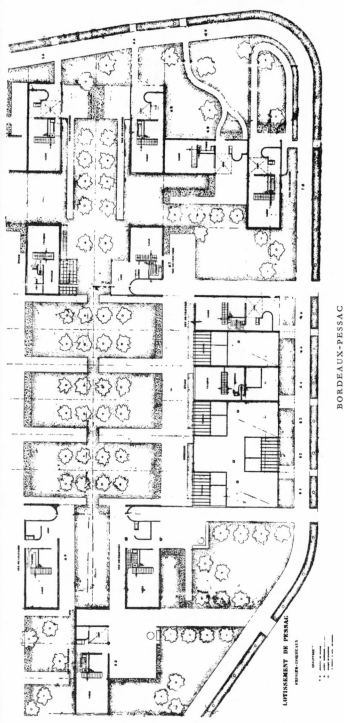

BORDEAUX-PESSAC

The first edition of this book had a profound effect on a large manufacturer of Bordeaux. It was decided to make a clean start. A noble conception of the aims of Industry, and those of Architecture, led this manufacturer to take a daring step. For the first time perhaps (as far as France is concerned), the pressing problems of Architecture, thanks to him, were solved in a modern spirit. Economy, sociology, aesthetics : a new solution, using new methods.

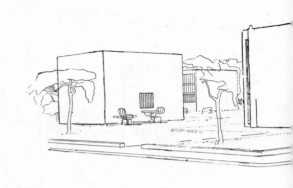

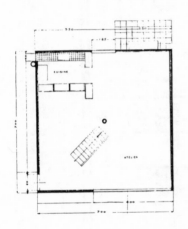

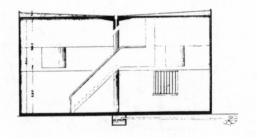

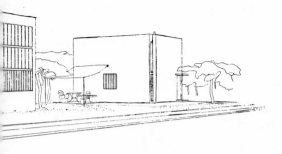

LE CORBUSIER AND PIERRE JEANNERET, 1924. MASS-PRODUCTION ARTISANS' DWELLINGS

The problem was that of housing artisans in a large and well-lit workshop; of lowering costs by the elimination as far as possible of partitions and doors, and by the reduction in the normal wall surfaces and heights of rooms—this by a little architectural management. The houses are built round a single hollow column of reinforced concrete. The walls are of compressed straw sheets (which have good insulating properties) rendered on the outside by 1½″ cement rendering thrown on under pressure by a " cement-gun," and plastered inside. There are only two doors to a house. The loft or upper floor, on the diagonal, allows the ceiling to be developed to its full extent (21 feet × 21 feet); the walls also are displayed to their full dimensions, and, moreover, the use of the diagonal creates an unexpected dimension: this little house, 21 feet square, gives along the diagonal the effect of a dimension of 30 feet in length.

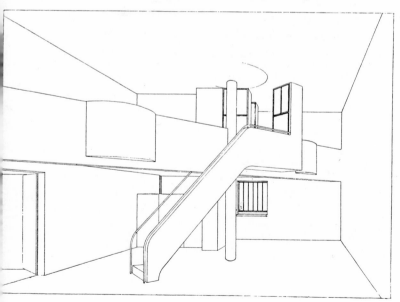

INTERIOR

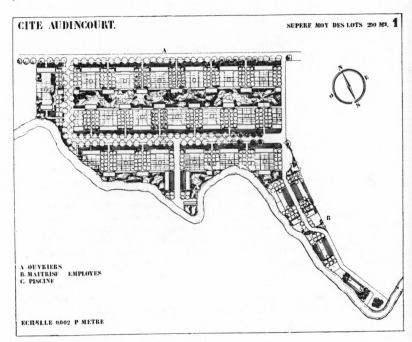

CITE AUDINCOURT.   SUPERF. MOY DES LOTS 200 M². 1

A. OUVRIERS
B. MAITRISE EMPLOYES
C. PISCINE

ECHELLE 0.002 P METRE

LE CORBUSIER AND PIERRE JEANNERET, 1924. HOUSING SCHEME

All the houses are constructed of standardized elements, forming a "cell" type. The plots are all equal, the arrangement regular. Architecture is very well able to express itself in a precise fashion.

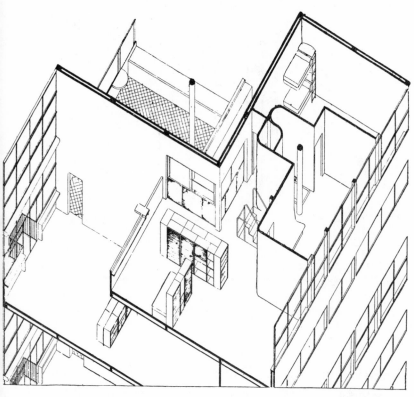

LE CORBUSIER AND PIERRE JEANNERET, 1924. ONE OF THE CELLS OF
A "FREEHOLD MAISONETTE" BLOCK (SEE EARLIER ILLUSTRATIONS).

A mass-production scheme, for the man of to-day : *the elements are architectural, the construction is entirely industrialized.*

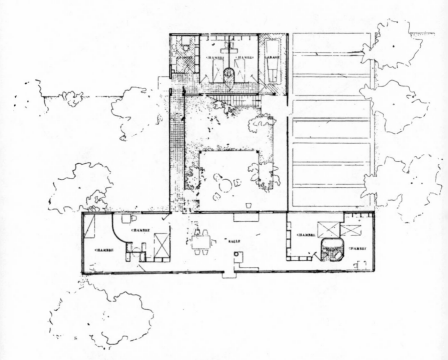

LE CORBUSIER AND PIERRE JEANNERET, 1925. A VILLA AT BORDEAUX.

Constructed of mass-production elements with the same machinery as was used for the garden-city houses at Pessac. Mass-production is not an obstacle to Architecture. On the contrary, it brings unity and perfection in detail and offers variety in the mass.

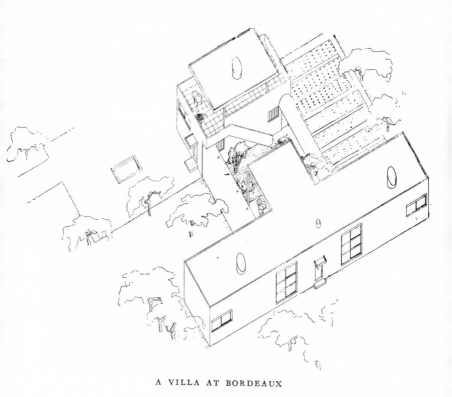

A VILLA AT BORDEAUX

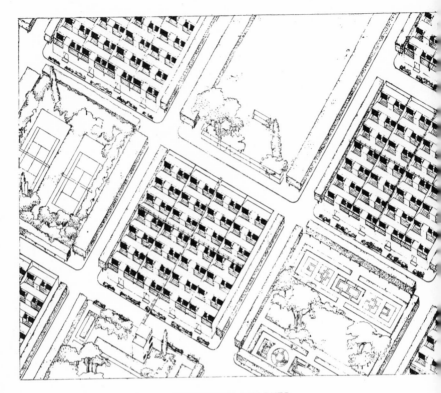

UNIVERSITY QUARTER

Attempts are made at enormous cost to build quarters for university students which may reproduce the poetry of the old buildings at Oxford. A costly poetry, disastrously so! The modern student is in any case inclined to protest against an old-world Oxford : an old-world Oxford is the dream of the modern Mæcenas, the donor of such a university quarter. What the student wants is a monk's cell, well lit and heated, with a corner from which he can look at the stars. He wants to find opportunity for games with his fellow-students at a stone's throw. His cell should be self-contained, as far as possible.

PLAN AND SECTIONS

Every student has a right to exactly the same type of cell : it would be invidious that the poor student should occupy a cell different from that of the rich student. There is the problem to be solved : the university-quarter-caravansary : each " cell " has its antechamber, its kitchen, its W.C., its living-room, its sleeping-loft, its roof-garden. Each student is cut off by walls from his neighbours. All the students can forgather on their sports-grounds or in the communal halls in the large buildings destined for communal services. We have to classify, form a type and settle the form of the cell and its elements. Economy. Efficiency. And Architecture? We can always achieve this when the problem is clear.
The university quarter is here conceived in a " shed " form ; a mode of con-struction which allows of indefinite expansion, with ideal lighting and an absence of constructional (and so costly) masses. The walls are mere fillings in light insulating materials.

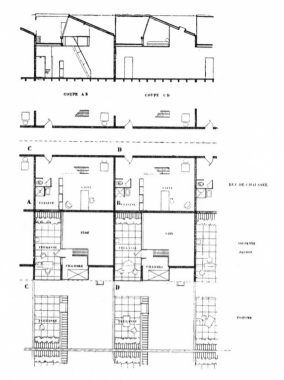

COUPE A B   COUPE C D

C   D

A   B

REZ-DE-CHAUSSÉE

SOUPENTE

JARDIN

TOITURE

PLAN AND SECTION

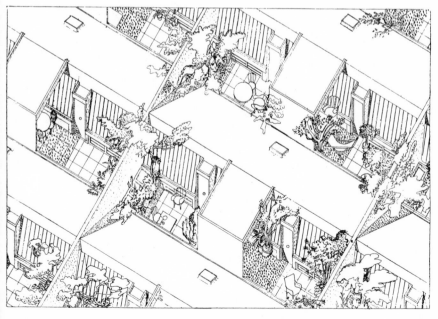

DETAIL OF THE TERRACE-GARDEN

longer be an archaic entity, heavily rooted in the soil by deep foundations, built " firm and strong," the object of the devotion on which the cult of the family and the race has so long been concentrated.

Eradicate from your mind any hard and fast conceptions in regard to the dwelling-house and look at the question from an objective and critical angle, and you will inevitably arrive at the " House-Tool," the mass-production house, available for everyone, incomparably healthier than the old kind (and morally so too) and beautiful in the same sense that the working tools, familiar to us in our present existence, are beautiful.

It will be beautiful, too, with the vitality that the artist's sensibility can give to its strict and pure organism.

But it is essential to create the right state of mind for living in mass-production houses.

Everybody, quite rightly, dreams of sheltering himself in a sure and permanent home of his own. This dream, because it is impossible in the existing state of things, is deemed incapable of realization and so provokes an actual state of sentimental hysteria ; to build one's own house is very much like making one's will. . . . When the time does arrive for building this house, it is not the mason's nor the craftsman's moment, but that moment in which every man makes *one* poem, at any rate, in his life. And so, in our towns and their outskirts, we have had during the last forty years not so much houses as *poems,* poems of an Indian summer, for a house is the crowning of a career . . . at that very moment when a man is sufficiently old

and worn by life to be the prey of rheumatism and of death . . .
and of crazy ideas.

A question of a new spirit :

I am 40 years old, why should I not buy a house for myself ?
for I need this instrument ; a house built on the same principles
as the Ford car I bought (or my Citroen, if I am particular).

Collaborators already consecrated to the task : big industry,
the specialized factories.

Collaborators who must be brought in : the suburban railway
lines, financial organizations, transformed Architectural Schools.

The aim : mass-production houses.

The coalition : one between architects and men of taste,
and the universal love of the home.

The executive : business concerns and true architects.

Irrefutable proof :

1. The *Salon de l'aviation ;*

2. Towns celebrated for beauty (the Venetian Procuracies,
the rue de Rivoli, the place des Vosges, la Carrière, Versailles,
etc. : all *mass-production*). For the mass-production house implies
general lines of a generous and ample sort. It necessitates a
minute study of every detail connected with the house, and a
close search for a standard, that is for a type. When this type
has been created, we are already at the gates of beauty (*cf.* the
motor-car, the liner, the lorry, the airplane). For the mass-

production house will impose unity in the various elements, windows, doors, methods of construction, materials. *Unity in detail and large general lines*—this was the demand, in Louis XIV's reign, in the muddled, congested, inextricable and uninhabitable Paris of that time, of a very intelligent *abbé*, Laugier, who busied himself with town-planning : *Uniformity in detail and variety in the general effect* (the exact opposite of what we do to-day : a mad variety in details, and a deadly uniformity in the setting out of our streets and towns).

Conclusion : We are dealing with an urgent problem of our epoch, nay more, with *the* problem of our epoch. The balance of society comes down to a question of building. We conclude with these justifiable alternatives : *Architecture or Revolution.*

A LOW-PRESSURE VENTILATING FAN

40,000 KILOWATT TURBINE FOR ELECTRICITY

ARCHITECTURE

OR

REVOLUTION

In every field of industry, new problems have presented themselves and new tools have been created capable of resolving them. If this new fact be set against the past, then you have revolution.

In building and construction, mass-production had already been begun; in face of new economic needs, mass-production units have been created both in mass and detail, and definite results have been achieved both in detail and in mass.

If this fact be set against the past, then you have revolution, both in the method employed and in the large scale on which it has been carried out.

The history of Architecture unfolds itself slowly across the centuries as a modification of structure and ornament, but in the last fifty years steel and concrete have brought new conquests, which are the index of a greater capacity for construction, and of an architecture in which the old codes have been overturned. If we challenge the past, we shall learn that "styles" no longer exist for us, that a style belonging to our own period has come about; and there has been a revolution.

Our minds have consciously or unconsciously apprehended these events and new needs have arisen, consciously or unconsciously. The machinery of Society, profoundly out of gear, *oscillates between an amelioration, of historical importance, and a catastrophe.*

The primordial instinct of every human being is to assure himself of a shelter.

The various classes of workers in society to-day no longer have dwellings adapted to their needs; neither the artisan nor the intellectual.

It is a question of building which is at the root of the social unrest of to-day; architecture or revolution.

IN every province of industry, new problems have arisen and have been met by the creation of a body of tools capable of dealing with them. We do not appreciate sufficiently the deep chasm between our own epoch and earlier periods; it is admitted that this age has effected a great transformation, but the really useful thing would be to draw up a parallel table of its activities—intellectual, social, economic and industrial—not only in relation to the preceding period at the beginning of the nineteenth century, but to the history of civilizations in general. It would quickly be seen that the tools that man has made for himself, which automatically meet the needs of society, and which till now had undergone only slight modifications in a slow evolution, have been transformed all at once with an amazing rapidity. These tools in the past were always *in man's hands*; to-day they have been entirely and formidably refashioned and for the time being are out of our grasp. The human animal stands breathless and panting before the tool that he cannot take hold of; progress appears to him as hateful as it is praiseworthy; all is confusion within his mind; he feels himself to be the slave of a frantic state of things and experiences no sense of liberation or comfort or amelioration. This is a great but critical period, above all of a moral crisis. To pass the crisis we must create the state of mind which can understand what is going on; the human animal must learn to use his tools. When this human animal has put on his new harness

THE EQUITABLE BUILDING, NEW YORK

and knows the effort that is expected from him, he will see that things have changed : and changed *for the better*.

One more word on the past. Our own epoch, that is to say the last fifty years only, confronts the ten ages that have gone before. During these earlier ages, man ordered his life in conformity with what people call a " natural " system ; he took his tasks upon his own shoulders and brought them to a satisfactory conclusion, bearing all the consequences of his own

STEEL CONSTRUCTION. THE STEEL CORPORATION

little enterprises: he rose with the sun, went to bed at dusk; he laid down his tools preoccupied with the task in hand and what he would begin on the morrow. He worked at home in a little booth, with his family around him. He lived like a snail in its shell, in a lodging made exactly to his measure; there was nothing to induce him to modify this state of things, which was indeed harmonious enough. The family life unfolded itself in a normal way. The father watched over his children in the cradle and later on in the workshop: effort and gain succeeded one another peacefully within the family order; and in this the family found its profit. Now when this is so, society is stable

"AMERICA"

A Racing Car of 250 h.p., capable of over 160 m.p.h.

and likely to endure. That is the story of ten ages of work organized within the family unit ; and the story too of every past age up to the middle of the nineteenth century.

But let us observe to-day the mechanism of the family. Industry has brought us to the mass-produced article ; machinery is at work in close collaboration with man ; the right man for the right job is coldly selected ; labourers, workmen, foremen, engineers, managers, administrators—each in his proper place ; and the man who is made of the right stuff to be a manager will not long remain a workman ; the higher places are open to all. Specialization ties man to his machine ; an absolute precision is demanded of every worker, for the article passed on to the next man cannot be snatched back in order to be corrected and fitted ; it must be exact in order that it may play, by that very reason, its part as a detailed unit which will be required to fit automatically into the assembling of the whole. The father no longer teaches his son the various secrets of his little trade ; a strange foreman directs severely and precisely the restrained and circumscribed tasks. The worker makes one tiny detail, always the same one, during months of work, perhaps during years of work, perhaps for the rest of his life. He only sees his task reach its finality in the finished work at the moment when it is passed, in its bright and shining purity, into the factory yard to be placed in a delivery-van. The spirit of the worker's booth no longer exists, but certainly there does exist a more collective spirit. If the workman is intelligent he will understand the final end of his labour, and this will fill him with a legitimate pride. When the *Auto* announces that such and such a car has reached 180 miles an hour, the workmen will gather together and tell one another : " *Our* car did that ! " There we have a moral factor which is of importance.

The eight hours day ! The three " eights " in the factory ! The shifts working in relays. This one starting at 10 p.m. and finishing at 6 a.m. ; another one ending at 2 p.m. Did our legislators think of that when they granted the eight hours day ? What is the man going to do with his freedom from 6 a.m. till 10 p.m. ; from 2 p.m. till night ? What becomes of the family under these conditions ? The lodging is there, you will say, to receive and welcome the human animal, and the worker is sufficiently cultivated to know how to make a healthy use of so many hours of liberty. But this is exactly what is *not* the case ;

NEW YORK

the lodging is hideous, and his mind not sufficiently educated to use all these hours of liberty. We may well say, then : Architecture or demoralization—demoralization and revolution.

Let us examine another point :

There is a formidable industrial activity at present in progress, which is inevitably and constantly at the back of our minds ; at every moment either directly, or through the medium of newspapers and reviews, we are presented with objects of an arresting novelty whose why and wherefore engrosses our minds, and fills us with delight and fear. All these objects of modern life create, in the long run, a modern state of mind. Bewilderment seizes us, then, if we bring our eyes to bear on the old and rotting buildings that form our snail-shell, our habitation, which crush us in our daily contact with them—

A CRANE

putrid and useless and unproductive. Everywhere can be seen machines which serve to produce something and produce it admirably, in a clean sort of way. The machine that we live in is an old coach full of tuberculosis. There is no real link between our daily activities at the factory, the office or the bank, which are healthy and useful and productive, and our activities in the bosom of the family which are handicapped at every turn. The family is everywhere being killed and men's minds demoralized in servitude to anachronisms.

Every man's mind, being moulded by his participation in contemporary events, has consciously or unconsciously formed certain desires ; these are inevitably connected with the family, an instinct which is the basis of society. Every man to-day realizes his need of sun, of warmth, of pure air and clean floors ; he has been taught to wear a shiny white collar, and women love fine white linen. Man feels to-day that he must have intellectual diversion, relaxation for his body, and the physical

SHIP'S COALERS ON THE RHINE

culture needed to recuperate him after the tension of muscle or brain which his labour—" hard labour "—brings. This mass of desires constitutes in fact a mass of *demands*.

Now our social organization has nothing ready which can answer these needs.

Another point : what are the conclusions of the *intellectuals* face to face with the actualities of modern life ?

The magnificent flowering of industry in our epoch has created a special class of intellectuals so numerous that it constitutes the really active stratum of society.

In the workshop, in the technical departments, in the learned Societies, in the banks and in the great stores, on newspapers and reviews, there are the engineers, the heads of departments, legal representatives, secretaries, editors, accountants who work out minutely, in accordance with their duty, the formidable things which occupy our attention : there are the men who design our bridges, ships and airplanes, who create our motors and turbines, who direct the workshops and yards, who are engaged in the distribution of capital and in accountancy, who do the purchasing of goods in the colonies or from the factory, who put forth so many articles in the Press on the modern production of so much that is noble and horrible, who record as on a chart the high-temperature curve of a humanity in labour, in perpetual labour, at a crisis—sometimes in delirium. All human material passes through their hands. In the end their observation must lead them to some conclusion. These people have their eyes fixed on the display of goods in the great shops that man has made for himself. The modern age is spread before them, sparkling and radiant . . . on the far side of the barrier ! In their own homes, where they live in a precarious ease, since their remuneration bears no real relation to the quality of their work, they find their uncleanly old snail-shell, and they cannot even think of having a family. If they do so there will begin the slow martyrdom that we all know. These people, too, claim their rights to a machine for living in, which shall be in all simplicity a *human* thing.

Both the worker and the intellectual are precluded from following their deepest instincts in regard to the family ; each and every day they make use of the brilliant and effective tools that the age has provided, but they are not enabled thereby to use them for themselves. Nothing could be more discouraging

or more irritating. Nothing is prepared. We may well say:
Architecture or Revolution.

Though modern society does not recompense its intellectuals judiciously, it still tolerates the old arrangements as to
property which are a serious barrier in the way of transforming
the town or the house. Established property rests on inheri-
tance and its highest aim is a state of inertia, of no change and
of maintaining the *status quo*. Although every other sort of

A TURBINE DISC FROM THE CREUSOT WORKS: 40,000 KILOWATTS.

human enterprise is subject to the rough warfare of competition, the landlord, ensconced in his property, escapes the common law in a princely fashion : he is a king. On the existing principle of property, it is impossible to establish a constructional programme which will hold together. And so the necessary building is not done. But if existing property arrangements were changed, and they are changing, it would be possible to build ; there would be an enthusiasm for building, and we should avoid Revolution.

The advent of a new period only occurs after long and quiet preparatory work.

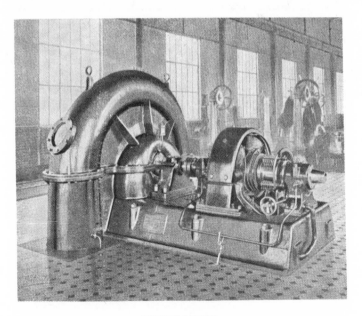

VENTILATORS

Hourly output 57,000 *cubic metres.*

A "BUGATTI" ENGINE

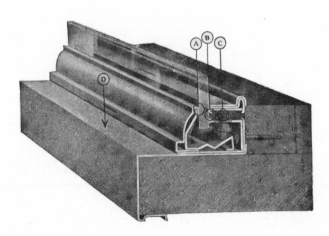

CHICAGO. CONSTRUCTION OF A WINDOW: INDUSTRIALIZATION

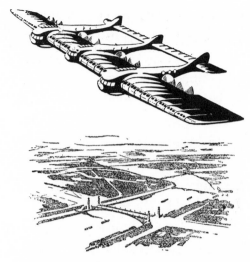

A FORECAST: THE AIRPLANE OF TO-MORROW

Industry has created its tools.

Business has modified its habits and customs.

Construction has found new means.

Architecture finds itself confronted with new laws.

Industry has created new tools: the illustrations in this book provide a telling proof of this. Such tools are capable of

A FACTORY (FREYSSINET & LIMOUSIN)

adding to human welfare and of lightening human toil. If these new conditions are set against the past, you have Revolution.

Business has modified its customs : it bears a heavy responsibility to-day : cost, time, solidity of the work. Engineers in numbers fill its offices, make their calculations, practise the laws of economy to an intensive degree, and seek to harmonize two opposed factors : cheapness and good work. Intelligence lies behind every initiative, bold innovations are demanded. The morality of industry has been transformed : big business is to-day a healthy and moral organism. If we set this new fact against the past, we have Revolution in method and in the scale of the adventure.

A HANGAR (FREYSSINET & LIMOUSIN)

Width 250 feet, height 150 feet, length over 900 feet.   The Nave of Notre Dame is 40 feet wide and about 107 feet in height.

A LARGE AIRSHIP HANGAR AT ORLY (FREYSSINET & LIMOUSIN)
Width 250 feet, height 170 feet, length over 900 feet.

Construction has discovered its methods, methods which in themselves mean a liberation that earlier ages had sought in vain. Everything is possible by calculation and invention, provided that there is at our disposal a sufficiently perfected body of tools, and this does exist. Concrete and steel have entirely transformed the constructional organisation hitherto known, and the exactitude with which these materials can be adapted to calculation and theory every day provides encouraging results, both in the success achieved and in their appearance, which recalls natural phenomena and constantly reproduces experiences realized in nature. If we set ourselves against the past, we can then appreciate the fact that new formulas have been found which only need exploitation to bring about (if we are wise enough to break with routine) a genuine liberation from the constraints we have till now been subjected to. There has been Revolution in methods of construction.

Architecture finds itself confronted with new laws. Construction has undergone innovations so great that the old " styles," which still obsess us, can no longer clothe it ; the materials employed evade the attentions of the decorative artist. There is so much novelty in the forms and rhythms furnished by these constructional methods, such novelty in arrangement and in the new industrial programmes, that we can no longer close our minds to the true and profound laws of architecture which are established on mass, rhythm and proportion : the " styles " no longer exist, they are outside our ken ; if they still trouble us, it is as parasites. If we set ourselves against the past, we are forced to the conclusion that the

THE "FIAT" WORKSHOPS AT TURIN WITH THE TESTING TRACK
ON THE ROOF

267

old architectural code, with its mass of rules and regulations evolved during four thousand years, is no longer of any interest ; it no longer concerns us : all the values have been revised ; there has been revolution in the conception of what Architecture is.

Disturbed by the reactions which play upon him from every quarter, the man of to-day is conscious, on the one hand, of a new world which is forming itself regularly, logically and clearly, which produces in a straightforward way things which are useful and usable, and on the other hand he finds himself, to his surprise, living in an old and hostile environment. This framework is his lodging ; his town, his street, his house or his flat rise up against him useless, hinder him from following the same path in his leisure that he pursues in his work, hinder him from following in his leisure the organic development of his existence, which is to create a family and to live, like every animal on this earth and like all men of all ages, an organized family life. In this way society is helping forward the destruction of the family, while she sees with terror that this will be her ruin.

There reigns a great disagreement between the modern state of mind, which is an admonition to us, and the stifling accumulation of age-long detritus.

The problem is one of adaptation, in which the realities of our life are in question.

Society is filled with a violent desire for something which it may obtain or may not. Everything lies in that : everything depends on the effort made and the attention paid to these alarming symptoms.

Architecture or Revolution.

Revolution can be avoided.

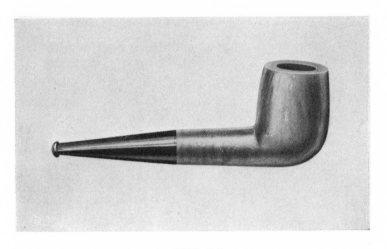

A BRIAR PIPE